Years Off My Life

Years Off My Life

THE MEMOIRS OF GENERAL OF THE SOVIET ARMY

A. V. Gorbatov

TRANSLATED BY

GORDON CLOUGH AND ANTHONY CASH

W · W · NORTON & COMPANY · INC ·

NEW YORK

357.092
G661

CONTENTS

Introduction

For thirty years or more the facts about Stalin's methods —the terror, the mass arrests, the torture, the labour camps —have been freely available in the West to anyone interested enough to listen and unbiased enough to accept plain evidence. By 1940 Arthur Koestler had explored once and for all, in *Darkness at Noon*, the reality of Communist involvement, trial and expiation. And long before the present Soviet rulers began to draw back the curtain slowly and cautiously on this tale of horror, the accounts of escaping refugees and defectors had enabled experts such as Dallin to compile, soon after the end of the Second World War, what amounted to handbooks of the Soviet Police State.

The more intense and catastrophic an experience, however, the more difficult it is for an outsider to achieve any direct understanding of it. The mind recoils and compassion is chilled. Too often, a morbid curiosity about individual cases takes the place of genuine sympathy. If this is true of a Western audience, it is very hard indeed to imagine the frame of mind of Soviet people when faced with the realities of Stalin's rule. We in the West have merely been subjected to a barrage of denials and told endlessly by Communist spokesmen from the late thirties onwards that those who stated the plain facts about life in the Soviet Union were at best dupes, and more likely evil-minded slanderers. The ordinary Soviet citizen, on the other hand, was given no inkling of the truth, and is still told little enough to this day. The gap between the high claims of Communism and the real facts was too great. An intermediate reality had to be created in which a peasant objecting to the forced collectivization of his newly-won land became a 'saboteur' and a 'class enemy', and a general fallen from favour turned into an enemy spy.

While Stalin's régime lasted his subjects had to grope blindly in the darkness of a nightmare for some rational account of the events that beset them. Now, they must attempt to reconstruct the past, and apportion blame, from facts half hinted at by their rulers, from disjointed shreds of history that are clearly incomplete and from whatever the authorities choose to let pass into print. Small wonder, therefore, that the memoirs of General Gorbatov should have created a sensation when extracts from them were published, in March, April and May, 1964, in the Moscow periodical *Novy Mir*.

General Gorbatov is a distinguished soldier whose successful career was interrupted by the wave of terror that turned against the Red Army in 1937, and swept away a very large number, perhaps the majority of the best senior officers. An as yet unknown number of them were shot, including two Red Army Marshals, Tukhachevski and Blyukher, while the rest were sent away, after interrogation and torture, to rot in forced labour camps. Gorbatov was both determined and lucky; he survived, to be released just before the German invasion in 1941, and he finished the war as Commandant of Berlin. It is the account of his experiences as a victim of the terror—the first such account to be published in the Soviet Union—that has attracted so much attention, not only in his own country but among students of Soviet affairs all over the world.

Yet General Gorbatov is not—far from it—an opponent
of the Communist régime. Indeed, one of the most astonish-
ing aspects of his book is that, throughout the terrifying
story of his arrest and imprisonment, and of the total dis-
organization of the Red Army in the opening stages of its
resistance against the Germans, he never once goes to the
heart of the matter in his search for the reasons that brought
him and the Red Army to the very brink of extinction. The
furthest he gets is, again and again, the question: 'Can the
leaders who unleashed this terror really have believed that
they were right? And if they did not, what caused such
suicidal madness?' Not once does it occur to him to speculate
about the possibility of radical flaws in the Communist
system. It is easy to be cynical about this failure to probe deep
enough. Clearly, had Gorbatov queried the foundations of
Communist ideology in his memoirs he would not have been
given permission to publish them. Yet I very much doubt
whether it is right to suspect General Gorbatov of suppres-
sing his deepest misgivings. He is too straightforward, too
honourable a man, almost a universal type—the keen,
talented, warm-hearted soldier, though gifted above the
average as a writer and with more than his share of humour
and shrewdness.

Another accusation, which applies equally to all those
who in a modern dictatorship take too narrow a view of
their allegiance and their civic duty, can be more fairly
made against him: that of failing to react until the interests
of the profession to which he had committed his life, of the
group to which he belonged, were threatened. From 1929
onwards the life of the Russian peasant faced with collectivization was a hell on earth. The terror that overran the
Soviet Union started in good earnest after the murder of
Kirov, possibly at Stalin's instigation, in December, 1934.

Gorbatov is the son of poor peasants for whom the acquisition of land was clearly the be-all and end-all of the Revolution. By the mid-thirties he was already a leading member of the Soviet *élite*. Yet in the extracts published in *Novy Mir* there is not a mention of collectivization, not a reference to the consequences of Kirov's murder, just a formal description of his military career until Stalin turned in 1937 against the Marshals and the Armed Forces.

The deeper reason for General Gorbatov's reticence, however, is his unquestioning dedication to the Soviet régime. In this sense his memoirs are not merely a life story of a kind unfamiliar to us in the West, but a first-rate historical document. From the time when we first meet Sanka Gorbatov at the age of ten in a setting worthy of Gorki to the moment of final victory over the Nazi invader it is Russian history from 1900 to 1945 as seen by those Russian peasants who were children at the turn of the century and to whom the Revolution gave opportunities of which they might not otherwise have dreamt. One may wonder whether young Sanka, with his native wit and courage, might not have made good under any régime, but that is certainly not how he and his like see it when they look back, from the eminence that they have reached today, at the harsh conditions in which their life began.

This makes it less difficult to understand the case of Cavalry Division Commander Gorbatov, arrested in 1938 and sentenced without the slightest justification, yet back serving his country in his old rank, unsparingly and fearlessly, only three years later.

Throughout his ordeal Gorbatov was sustained by the fact that in spite of every cruelty and every indignity he had never confessed and never implicated others. General Gorbatov, as his story shows, is a broadminded and surpris-

ingly tolerant man. Yet, even with his experience of what
Soviet Police methods and conditions in the forced labour
camps could do to break down self-respect, he never lost
his sense of outrage at the fact that so many otherwise
honourable and courageous men should have confessed to
imaginary crimes and dragged down others merely to save
their own skins.

This sense of outrage is shared by much of the younger
generation in the Soviet Union today, particularly by young
intellectuals. Those under the age of thirty have not felt the
pressures that forced most of their elders to conform or
perish. They only know that virtually all who were active
under Stalin and survived must either bear some responsibility for the blood and the suffering, or have lost any claim
to self-respect by their bogus confessions; both, indeed, more
often than not. They cannot understand. And to them,
General Gorbatov and those few who, like him, refused to
buy survival at the price of human dignity are all that
stands between them and a cynical withdrawal of belief in
the possibility of ordinary decency, let alone honour.

Alexander Lieven
September 1964

Part One

ONE

Childhood

I was born in 1892. Mine was a peasant family, very poor, and there were ten children. Both my parents were pious and devout, and they were hard workers. My father neither drank nor smoked nor swore. He was not a large man, in fact he was rather thin and sickly, but we children knew how strong he was; we often felt the weight of his hand when he thought he should 'teach us a lesson'. He taught us conscience. My mother worried incessantly about how she was going to feed and clothe and find shoes for us all. Only the eldest boy and the eldest girl ever got new clothes; the rest of us wore their old ones as we grew. We were always quite well turned out, though. Mother mended the holes and tears and nobody minded the odd patch. Mother also did the housework, kept the garden and looked after the cow and the horse. Of course, we all helped. Even seven-year-old Anya could call herself a worker as she kept an eye on the three youngest.

Bread was always a problem. We had to be sparing with bread because our own grain never lasted us through the year. Mother had to measure each piece carefully as she cut it: they must all be exactly the same size. We were a peaceful family on the whole, but such things sometimes started a fight. Then father's heavy hand would have to intervene. We were always hungry, no matter how hard we worked. Our milk, cream and butter all went to market.

Every year we killed a calf, but that had to go to market too.

Because we could never afford to buy good horses they never lasted more than a year or two with us. At that time a really good cart-horse cost sixty or seventy roubles; we bought ours for ten or fifteen, and once we got one for seven. They were already well past their prime by then. When they died I used to help my father skin them. This had to be done very carefully as each blemish from the knife lowered the value of the skin, and for a clean skin we could get three or four roubles towards another horse.

Around Pakhotino, our village, and the villages nearby there was very little work during the winter and every male over twelve years of age took a seasonal job away from home cleaning sheep skins. They were away until Shrovetide, and sometimes for a few weeks of Lent as well; the longer the work went on the better everyone was pleased, because it meant more money and more wool, combed from the skins, to bring home. All the women and girls who did not work in the factories in Shuya, the nearby town, spent the autumn spinning the wool and knitting mittens for sale.

Beyond Pakhotino to the west were the woods and marshes. When spring came we all went harvesting for berries and mushrooms. The best of them, of course, were sent to market; only the tiny berries and the worm-eaten mushrooms found their way to our table. In the autumn we picked cranberries, and after the first frosts there were rose-hips. The horse and the cow needed their fodder too and we cut hay wherever we could find it in the woods and meadows. We even gathered sedge in the marshes and carried it home, walking for nearly a mile waist-deep in water. We made as much hay as we could and sold what we did not need. In such ways every one of us did his best to earn an extra kopek or two for the family purse.

I started my three years of schooling in the autumn of 1899. The parish school was about three miles from Pakho-tino, and to get there we had to go through two woods and two small villages. There was a legend about one of those woods—that years ago someone had hanged himself from a tree. We ran very fast through it and burst into the village beyond, shouting with relief and sheer joy at being alive.

Between that village, Ovsyannitsa, and the next one there was a smooth round hummock. It was said that a boat loaded with gold was buried under it, although what a boat was doing there was something I could never understand. As we passed the spot we used to make up stories about finding the gold and discuss what we would buy with it. In the autumn we usually decided on some good strong shoes. In the winter it was fur coats and mufflers and warm fur boots. Sometimes, though, we agreed that we would most like to build a house that was full of nooks and crannies, where we could all play hide-and-seek.

By the summer of 1901 I had learned to read. I found somewhere a little book about ferns, and when I had read the chapter about how a fern flowers I had a passionate desire to witness this strange occurrence for myself. I knew there were many ferns in the nearby woods, and Midsummer Eve was only three days away. I went off into the woods by myself, looked around a bit, noted a likely little hillock where I could watch from, and on my way back blazed the bushes so that I would have no trouble finding the place again in the dark. On Midsummer Eve itself, as soon as it was dark, I took the small brass cross from the ikon stand in the corner, hid it inside my shirt and slipped out of the house unobserved.

I found the trail easily and was soon at the hillock I had chosen. I was trembling with fright but I told myself that if the Evil One had made me come this far it must mean that the ferns really would flower that night. With the end of the little cross I drew three circles round the hillock, carefully following the instructions in my book. Then I stood on the top, bowed deliberately to the four corners of the earth, not forgetting to genuflect each time as well, and sat down to wait, holding the cross in a firm grip in my left hand and stretching out my right hand to catch the flower the instant it bloomed. I knew I would miss it if I was not ready.

Suddenly I became aware that it was growing light. I did not dare glance round for fear that this was one of the Evil One's tricks to make me miss the flower. But as I waited, and it grew lighter and lighter, I had to admit that this was the dawn and that I had been fast asleep. There was no point in waiting any longer. I stepped across the circle and ran out of the wood without a backward glance. When I reached the stream at the bottom of the meadow I stopped to catch my breath. Calm again, I looked back.

The sun was rising through the trees and on the grass the dew began to sparkle. Depressed by the fears and strains of the night, my soul was now suffused with a pure joy I had never known before. I knew now that the Evil One had no more power over me. I flopped down in the grass and slept.

I had not been missed at home, but when later in the day I heard my father shout, 'Where's the cross from the ikon stand?' my heart sank to my heels. I had lost it! If anyone found out it was me, and what I had used it for, there would be a terrible row. I dashed back to the wood and after a short search found where I had dropped it. That evening it was back in its place. 'Where on earth has it been?' asked everyone in surprise. But they didn't ask me, and I said nothing.

I never found out about the fern, whether I had been
asleep when it flowered or whether I had just missed it. I
was angry with the book and tore it up. That was my last
childhood fantasy of sudden wealth, born of the constant
poverty we lived in.

I finished my schooling in the spring of 1902 and proudly
carried home my certificate of good conduct and progress.
My mother wept for joy, and all the family gathered round
and congratulated me. Leaving school laid on me new
duties, however. My two elder brothers, Nikolai and Ivan,
and my elder sister, Tanya, were already working in the
nearby town; the one who was just out of school must
become the parents' chief workmate. That autumn my
father left to find work cleaning sheep skins, and in October
we had a letter from him to say that he had got a job in a
village called Olshanka, near Khvalynsk in Saratov
province, and that Nikolai was to give up his job in Shuya
and bring Sanka (that was my nickname) on the steamer to
join him.

I remember mother came to see us off at the quay where
we boarded the steamer that was to take us down the
Klyazma, the Oka and the Volga to Khvalynsk. We arrived
at Khvalynsk as the sun was coming up, and disembarked.
On the bank the melon sellers had huge piles of their wares
on display and we bought the two biggest water melons we
could find for three kopeks. After our breakfast we shouldered
our knapsacks, picked up our bags of tools (hooks, paring
knives, carding combs, etc.) and set off down the rain-
sodden road for the twelve-mile walk to Olshanka. The going
was difficult and the bags were heavy but fortunately we
were soon overtaken by a peasant with a horse and cart.
He was going to Olshanka and he let me ride up the hill

in the cart. When we reached the top he let Nikolai climb up with all the luggage as well.

In Olshanka we found there was little work for us after all. Two other men had beaten us to it. By the middle of winter all the skins were cleaned and there was no more to do. We pooled our meagre earnings. Clearly the wool we had saved to take home would now have to be sold in Olshanka, even though we would get next to nothing for it there, if we were to have enough money to pay the twenty-five roubles (a lot of money in those days) for our board and lodging and buy our tickets home. In any case it looked as if we would arrive home empty-handed.

Father, normally a man of the sternest character, was on this occasion so distressed that he even consulted Nikolai and myself about what we should do. Nikolai said straight out that we should leave at night, under cover of darkness, thus keeping both the wool and the twenty-five roubles and having something to show for our efforts when we got home. Fortunately our passes were in our possession and not the landlord's. Feeling bold I agreed with Nikolai's plan, but father was hesitant. He had never in his life done a dishonest thing and was inclined to sell the wool and pay the landlord what we owed him.

'But the landlord is a rich man,' Nikolai insisted. 'He knows how poor we are. Surely he'll understand.'

Indeed there did seem to be no other way out and by our joint efforts father was eventually persuaded. We hired a cart, loaded it up, and left stealthily that night. On the quayside at Syzran father 'borrowed' another traveller's six-year-old son and bought a quarter-ticket for me. I kept out of sight because I was already old enough to need a half. We thanked the boy's father and gave him three bread rolls.

Nikolai and I were worried that the landlord might have

sent the police after us, and when the steamer cast off we breathed a sigh of relief and cheered up. Father, however, was silent for the whole voyage. He felt that he had acted dishonestly and it upset him. In this he was unusual; such 'crimes' against the property rights of the rich had become so much a normal part of the peasant way of life that any guilt they might have carried had almost completely disappeared. For most of us our only worry was whether we would get away with it.

For example, not far from our village the forest began and all the villagers collected brushwood there. Sometimes, however, we managed to cut down a dead tree, which was strictly forbidden and if discovered could lead to a lot of trouble with the forester. We would chop it up into logs, stack them in the cart, and carefully camouflage them with brushwood. It was always a frightening moment when we passed the forester's hut on the river bank just by the bridge with such a load.

On one occasion, when we had finished the spring work in the fields and the garden and there was a little time to spare, my father and I set off into the forest to collect wood and were lucky enough to find three dry logs. We loaded them on the cart and covered them with brushwood. My father told me to take the load home, have a bite to eat and come back, while he stayed on and worked.

There were two ways home—round by the road or across the meadow. Across the meadow was quicker but there was a ditch to negotiate, and my father sent me off with strict instructions to go round by the road. I naturally promised to do exactly that, but as I left the forest I decided to save myself the extra mile and swung off the road into the meadow. When I came to the ditch I found the best place to cross and gave the horse a good smack on the rump. He leaped forward, there was a squeak of splintering wood, and he lurched to a halt. One wheel broke, and with a crunch the cart settled sideways in the bottom of the ditch.

I was so horrified that for a moment I could not think what to do. To right the cart I would have to unload the three logs in full view of the forester whose hut was only three hundred yards away. The thought of facing my father was even more frightening, so I decided to abandon the cart and ride back to the village. Just as I was unharnessing the horse I saw my father striding across the meadow towards me. He had evidently not trusted my promise and had come to the edge of the forest to see for himself which route I took.

I stood rooted to the spot, unable to move. Then, when he was not more than a few yards from me, I took to my heels and fled back towards the forest. From the shelter of a bush I saw my father finish unharnessing the horse and ride off towards the village. I waited to see whether the forester would come out of his hut. He did not appear, however, and as after a long time there was still no sign of my father returning I wandered off into the forest, thoroughly miserable. I fell down on my knees, weeping bitterly, and pleaded with God and all the saints whose names I could remember to soften my father's heart. The truth is I was terrified of a thrashing. A kind of fascination forced me to go back and see what my father was doing.

Behind my bush again I saw that father had borrowed a new wheel and, using an axle tree as a lever, he was fitting it on the cart. I wanted to rush out of hiding and go to him, help him, beg his forgiveness—but I stayed where I was, held by my fear. Soon the wheel was on. Father had lightened the load and put the horse between the shafts again and was all set to pull the cart out of the ditch. I said to myself, 'I'm going to him now, whatever happens,' but with a sudden lurch the cart was clear. Before I could move father had loaded the cart again and started back towards the village.

Only after dark did I dare return. I spent the rest of the night in the shed, praying. The sun was already high in the sky when I dozed off.

I saw my father as soon as I entered the house. He got up and came towards me. I stopped and waited for the blow. Just then a voice wailed out in the street, 'Scythes and sickles! Scythes and sickles!' and we heard a cart rumble to a stop.

My father went out quickly. Ten minutes later he returned carrying two scythes and two sickles which he was fingering with loving care. 'I got them on credit,' he said to my mother, a pleased grin on his face. 'And he wasn't lying, either. He said they were made in Austria, and look at the writing on them—it's different from ours.'

All I had had was one severe look! He had not raised a finger against me. Why was this? I asked my mother later and she told me they had not slept a wink all night for fear of what had happened to me. So it had not been God and his holy saints, after all, who had softened my father's heart —it had been my mother!

That autumn my father looked for work nearer home, so as not to waste money travelling a great distance. He found a job not far from Ryazan. Nikolai had learned from hard experience and this time he refused point-blank to give up his job in Shuya. My father and I went alone.

Cleaning sheep skins is hard, unpleasant and filthy work. First we would go round and collect a batch of skins— usually about a hundred and fifty at a time—from the local peasants. We soaked the skins in a stream to make it easier to clean off all the dirt and dung, then we carried them to a shed and with a sharp knife pared off the lumps of flesh that still clung to them. There were several huge vats of water in the shed. Into these we poured half-hundred-weight bags of flour, dipped the skins in them and left them to ferment. The stench in the shed was murderous. It permeated every scrap of clothing and every pore of one's skin. It made breathing so difficult that men unused to the work could stay no more than ten minutes at a time in the curing room before they had to dash outside for fresh air. It took us weeks to get rid of the smell from our bodies. You can always sniff out from a long way off a man who works with sheep skins.

This year, after we had collected our second batch of skins, my father suddenly felt sick and told me to take them down to the stream by myself. It was an extremely cold day —exactly how cold I cannot say, because at that time we had not even heard of a thermometer in our village—and I had to cut a hole in the ice and dip the skins through it. The work went slowly as I had to keep stopping to thaw out my numb hands. Gradually my fingers lost their grip until, as I was nearing the end of my task, they let one skin slip and the current carried it away under the ice.

I was well aware what a loss this was. A raw skin cost us fifty or sixty kopeks, and we could make thirteen kopeks' profit on a finished white skin, seventeen on a tanned skin, and up to twenty-five on a black one. I wondered how on earth I was going to tell father. By the time I got back to the shed with the skins I had decided to say nothing. Father counted them carefully, then counted them again. There could be no doubt that one was missing and I had to confess that I had lost it. He beat me very hard and at first I bore it patiently. After all I deserved my punishment. But after the third thrashing I told him in anger that I would run away, for which he thrashed me again.

Next morning my father counted the skins again and gave me another furious hiding, so I decided to go home. I grabbed a bucket and announced that I was going to fetch water. Safely out of the yard and round the corner, I dropped the bucket and set off in the direction of Ryazan, intending to follow the narrow-gauge railway from there through Vladimir to Shuya and home to the village and my mother. I hadn't a kopek in my pocket, my clothes did nothing to keep out the cold, and I was two hundred miles from home, but these things were nothing beside my determination.

The railway had been swept away by avalanches in places and the going was very bad. I was forced to take the main road, which put a lot of distance on my journey. I should have been able to do a dozen miles a day but the daylight hours were short and I was afraid to travel at night with wolves about. Most nights I managed to get accommodation in a village, though it was given unwillingly because of the strong smell of sheep skins that still hung about me.

On Epiphany Eve it was already dark as I approached a village. The moon was bright that night, however, and there were a lot of youngsters out in the street, talking and playing. I went from door to door, asking for a bed, but the house-wives had all got their houses spick and span for the festival and no one wanted my sour presence. As the last one turned me away, bitterly insulted, frozen and weak with hunger, I began to cry with utter loneliness.

I noticed a group of buildings standing a short way beyond the village and set off dejectedly towards them. They turned out to be bathhouses. The doors were padlocked, but from the steam seeping under the doors I could see there was warmth at least inside. Then I found a door ajar, went in

and found myself in a changing room. There was no one
about. Another door led into the main bathroom. No one
there either. In the dark I groped my way to a bench. After
gnawing for a while on a frozen crust of bread that I found
in my pocket, I lay down in my clothes with my hat under
my head and fell blissfully asleep.

A crash woke me, like some heavy object falling off a shelf.
'A house goblin!' I thought in panic. A little light from the
moon came through a tiny window and to my horror I
could make out the figure of a man, lying on the floor across
the doorway with one leg up on a bench. I was terrified; the
window was too small to escape through and the door was
blocked by the man! Beside myself with fright I leapt over
the body and out of the door. I slammed it behind me and
fled towards the village, screaming for help. People were still
strolling about in the street and at my cries they came running. What was the matter? they asked. Through my tears
I blurted out what had happened—and they burst into
laughter! It turned out that they had found a frozen traveller
on the road that night and had dumped him in the bathhouse to thaw out. One of them took pity on me and put me
up for the night.

When I finally reached Pakhotino and my mother saw me
coming in the door she was speechless for a moment. Then
she threw herself on me, weeping and saying over and over
again, 'Sanka, you're alive! My darling son, are you really
alive?' Father had written to her as soon as I had left,
saying no one knew where I was, and they had both been
mourning me for dead since then. Even my father, when he
came home later, did not scold me at all. He drew me to
him, stroked my hair and murmured, 'Why did you do it,
Sanka?' That was the last time he ever referred to the
episode.

I did not go back to Ryazan but spent the rest of that winter racking my brains to think of a way to augment the family budget. In our village the girls spent the long winter evenings together spinning wool and knitting mittens and gloves for sale. When they all came to our house it was my job to splinter some matchwood for a light and set it up and see that it burned well and evenly and that the ash dropped neatly into a bowl of water. The girls were quite happy with this type of light. In fact they were so skilful that they could knit in the dark without dropping a single stitch.

One such evening an idea occurred to me. The things they knitted were normally sold in nearby Shuya for twelve or thirteen kopeks a pair. Supposing instead of selling them in Shuya we took them by sledge to places further away where there was little knitting done? Surely they would fetch a much better price? Next morning I suggested this to my mother. She agreed in principle but reckoned that to do any good we would have to take them forty-five or fifty miles away, and that was too far for a small boy (I was small—I didn't start growing properly till I was sixteen) to drag a sledge, and the volume of goods did not justify taking the horse; that would cut the profit.

The idea of earning something by my own efforts fascinated me, however, and besides I was already looking forward to the journey. I pointed out to my mother that for a 'small boy' who had recently walked the best part of two hundred miles on his own it was hardly a stiff proposition to pull a few mittens forty-five miles on a sledge. Finally, with much sighing and complaining, she agreed and we got down to planning the trip. We worked out how many pairs I should take and what I should charge. According to my calculations, and I was good at arithmetic, we would clear three roubles more than we could get for the same goods in Shuya. That was almost as much as Nikolai earned in a week. My clothes were patched and the sledge put in order and we borrowed another seventy pairs of mittens from the neighbours in addition to what we had ourselves. At last I was ready.

I remember that day very clearly. My mother and I set out together. She took me the first part of the journey with the horse and I sat proudly on the sledge beside the two large sackfuls of mittens. After ten miles or so we unhitched the sledge and said our goodbyes. My mother wept as she gave me her blessing, sobbing, 'Sanka, you will come back, won't you? And with God's help you'll bring some money back, won't you?' It was very hard for me to leave her, in fact I howled as soon as she and the horse had disappeared round a bend in the road. I loved my mother very much. Then I adjusted the load on the sledge, hitched the harness round my shoulders and set off on my journey.

The going was quite good and I soon covered the remaining six or seven miles to the first large village, where I put up for the night. Next morning at the market there was a big demand for my mittens. With some trepidation I raised my price by three kopeks a pair—and sold half a sackful! Much encouraged I set off for the next big village that had a market. At each small settlement I passed through on the way I cried my wares like a real pedlar: 'Mittens! Fine mittens for sale!' I stopped from time to time, displayed my goods and, growing bolder, gradually put up the price by a further four kopeks. Business was equally brisk in the next market village.

I was now some forty miles from home, and could easily have sold the remaining pairs on my way back, but I decided to go another few miles further on, where there was another large village, and sell them there. It was the right decision because, with a further five kopeks on the price, I sold another sixty pairs. With only twenty pairs left I turned back for home. I had sold out completely by the time I got home, to the great delight of my mother and the family. The neighbours came round: 'Just think!' they said, 'such a small boy but such a good worker!' In a week exactly I had earned seven roubles and ten kopeks.

Three days later I was fitting myself out for another trip. Nearly all our own mittens had gone on the first trip, so we bought most of my stock from the neighbours. The day I left there was a hard frost, with a driving wind and intermittent snowstorms. Parting from my mother was not so hard this time. She even managed a little smile as she saw me off.

I was deep in the forest and miles from any houses when two wolves stepped out on to the path a little way in front of me. I stopped dead, terrifyingly conscious of my helpless position. The wolves, too, had stopped and were looking in my direction. They could almost have been discussing what to do about me. After what seemed an age they loped off and disappeared in the forest. Still I stood rooted to the spot, undecided whether to go on or return to the last village I had passed. It was pride that made me go on eventually, but for some time after that I cast fearful glances from side to side, until I was overtaken by a horse and cart and got a lift to the next village.

With experience my confidence increased and business went better and better. In that second seven-day trip I took nine roubles forty kopeks and when I got home I found I was the talk of the district. A steady stream of relations and neighbours came to the house to gape at the 'expert'. My mother was proud indeed of her Sanka, and there was respect in the eyes of my brothers and sisters. I felt like a hero.

The Russo-Japanese war began and the call went out for
more soldiers. My elder sister, Tanya, had married a year
ago a very nice man from the village. That summer she saw
him off to the front. The whole family was saddened by this
and my mother wanted to let her two brothers who worked
in Ivanovo and Kokhma know the news. I was the obvious
choice for messenger. I left the house early one morning
with my uncles' addresses on a piece of paper tucked into
the lining of my hat. As it was summer I ran barefoot.

It was thirty miles to Ivanovo and as it was already
evening when I arrived I decided to spend the night there.
My news, however, was received with complete indifference.
They even asked me, 'Was it worth running so far just to tell
us that? Some people have been at the front for weeks
already.' I considered this to be a base insult to the family
and refused to stay for the night. Although I was very tired
I covered the remaining eight miles to Kokhma that
evening.

At Kokhma my Uncle Pavel welcomed me warmly. He
expressed his sympathy for my sister Tanya and asked me to
convey his wishes for her husband's safe and speedy return.
He also showed great surprise at my endurance; it was no
joke for a small boy to cover thirty-eight miles in a day, he
said, and he was proud to have me in his house. In the
morning he and his wife gave me a silver ten-kopek piece. I
thanked them for everything, gripped the coin firmly in my
hand and set out for home.

As I was passing through a village on my way I noticed a
huge cherry orchard in the garden of the priest's house.
I could not resist the temptation to hop over the fence and
have some. Just behind the fence was a pile of windfalls and
I sat down on the grass to tuck in. The cherries were beauti-
fully sweet but gave off a rather sharp scent. When I had

eaten quite a few I began to feel sleepy and a little dizzy as
well. I have no idea how long I slept, but when I woke up my
head felt strangely heavy. 'What's this?' I thought. 'Am I
ill? I've come no more than six miles and I need a nap!'
I decided to get home as fast as I could in case there was
something wrong with me, but about five miles further on
I suddenly discovered I no longer had my ten-kopek piece
and had to go back and find it. When at last I reached home
I gave my mother the money and told her and father
everything that had happened on the trip, even about the
cherries. 'You're a fine one!' said my mother as she thanked
me. 'Those cherries had fermented. They'd turned into
alcohol. Someone had dumped them behind the fence so that
the hens wouldn't eat them. No wonder you woke up with a
thick head!'

That winter my father again tried to get work fairly near
home, but when he wrote it was to say he had found a job
a hundred miles away. He gave me detailed instructions
about how to reach the place, with the names of all the
villages I would pass through, adding that somewhere
about half-way there was a large wood in the middle of
which was a healing stream with a chapel beside it; I was to
wash in the stream and drink the water.

My mother started with me to see me on my way. 'It's a
six-day journey, Sanka,' she said, 'and if I come the first bit
with you it will be less far for you to walk on your own.' On
the third day I came to the wood my father had mentioned.
A path led away from the road and there, as he had said,
was the chapel and a clear, cold stream running beside it. I
obeyed his orders to the letter and solemnly washed in the
stream, drank and said a prayer. Thinking it would be a

good idea to make a small offering as well I walked round the chapel looking for the collecting bowl.

It was a large chapel, built of massive logs, the door secured with an enormous padlock, but there was no sign of a bowl. Such chapels usually had one hanging from the wall. I supposed there was none here because in a remote place like this the risk of theft would be great. Then I noticed that one of the grille-covered windows had a pane missing. Up on tiptoe, I peered inside. To my astonishment the floor just under the window was covered with coins, mostly copper coins but with some silver ten-kopek pieces among them. It was a common saying in our family, 'You don't chuck money on the floor.' Yet here was this floor just littered with money! I grew thoughtful.

I took off my knapsack and sat down to have a rest. The woman of the house where I had stayed the night before had given me a piece of bread which I now ate, washed down with some more of the healing water. Soon I was ready to go, but could not bring myself to leave without one more glance through the window. All that money! Sighing deeply, I set off again, lost in thought.

The vision of the money just lying about on the chapel floor nagged me all day. 'Surely God knows,' I said to myself, 'how much we need that money? Surely he would forgive me if I took some, if I took just a little? Maybe if I lit a candle. . . .?' I resolved to light a candle and say a prayer as soon as I had the opportunity, and meanwhile got down to thinking about how to reach the money.

Before I was aware of it I was out of the wood and approaching a village. Darkness was falling and it was time to find a place for the night. From bitter experience I knew that it was no good asking at a house that looked rich or at a

house that looked too poor; at a rich house I would be turned
away automatically, and at a poor house I would get nothing
to eat, for the simple reason that they probably had nothing
to eat themselves. I picked out a house that looked suitable.
A pleasant looking, middle-aged woman was standing by
the door. She asked me where I was from and where I was
going, and I said I was from near Palekh (I thought more
people would have heard of that than of Pakhotino) and that
I was heading for Lopatino, some forty-five miles away, to
help my father with the sheep skins. She was evidently
sorry for me and went inside to tell her husband that I was
staying the night. He said nothing but gave me a cursory
glance as I followed his wife inside, and then turned back to
the pair of felt boots he was sewing up. The woman made me
an enormous meal and told me I could sleep on the bench
by the door, but although I was worn out I could not sleep
a wink for thinking about that money and how I was going
to lay my hands on it.

After a while the man finished his sewing and began
caulking the seams of the boots with cobbler's wax. I watched
him for a time and was suddenly struck with an idea:
cobbler's wax was just the job! Feigning sleep, I made a
careful note of where he put the wax when he had finished.
Very early in the morning, when the woman had lit a lamp
and gone out to milk the cow, I quietly dressed myself, took
a piece of the wax and hid it in my knapsack. I hung around
for a bit in case I should get something more to eat, and was
not disappointed. She gave me a large bowl of milk to drink
and wrapped up a piece of potato pie for me to eat on the
road. Thanking her warmly I left the house.

I walked on down the street past several houses, then
doubled back down a side road and headed for the chapel
once more. A broken-down cart by the roadside gave me

another idea; I scraped up a little of the axlegrease that was oozing from the hub and trotted on.

As I approached the chapel I began to feel twinges of doubt about the rightness of what I was doing. This might, after all, be a temptation sent by the Evil One. It might be a mortal sin! But then I remembered how badly we needed the money, how sad my father must be, earning so little and living in a strange place, and how pleased my mother would be to have a rouble or two to spend on things for the house. Soon my confidence was wholly restored.

For some time I remained kneeling in prayer. Then I took a drink from the holy spring, cut a suitably tall birch sapling, smeared the end of it with wax and grease, and set to work.

The first coin—a five-kopek piece—stuck so firmly to the wax and came out so easily that I became convinced God was with me. I worked quickly, picking up copper coins mainly but also one or two silver ones, and the clear spot on the floor grew larger. It became more and more difficult to reach the coins, and as I strained after a silver ten-kopek piece that lay just beyond my reach I suddenly panicked— what if my greed began to anger God? I jumped back from the window and threw the sapling as far as I could into the bushes. Quickly I cleaned the grease and wax off the coins and counted them. Two roubles and eight kopeks! I gasped. Muttering a quick prayer and reaffirming my promise to light a candle, I returned to the village.

The work had taken me most of the day and I realised I would have to spend another night in the same village. I had no conscience about stealing the wax—a whole pound of wax cost only one kopek—but even so I kept to the back lanes and found a place to stay at the opposite end of the village. I had enough worries without inviting any more. The main problem was going to be concealing my new-found wealth from father. I wanted to give it all to my mother.

Father was pleased to see me when I arrived, but however hard I tried I could not keep my secret from him for long. Then the questioning began: where did it come from? how did I get it? why had I taken it? and so on. I had to tell everything—and I got the thrashing of my life. 'You worthless wretch!' yelled my father as he hit me. 'How dare you steal money from God? Take it back where you got it from immediately!'

I boiled over at this. 'But it's three days there and three days back,' I protested, 'and who is going to help you meanwhile? Anyway you wouldn't know whether I'd really thrown it back or was just saying so. If we're putting it back at all let's do so on our way home.'

When I answered him back like this my father flew into an even worse rage. His hand was raised again but I shouted, 'Touch me once more and I'm off! I'll run away!'

Things were all right after that and the subject was dropped. I suppose my father remembered what had happened the year before.

That was not the end of it, however. When we had collected our hundred and fifty skins and were ready to start the fermenting process, we found we were short of a rouble for flour and the baker would give us no more credit. I promptly suggested taking a rouble from my money. At this my father exploded again: '*Your* money? What do you mean—*your* money? That money belongs to God!' He was about to cuff me again, but then I think he remembered my threat. In the end, of course, still complaining, he was forced to take it, and later we were even more hard up and had to spend the rest. Father stubbornly maintained it was a sin and said we must put it all back on our way home. He too made a vow to light a candle, as I had done.

Looking back on it now, I can see that I had already lost all sense of guilt about the affair. I was just angry with myself for not having changed the coins for notes. Two rouble notes would have been easy to hide and I could have got them back to mother with no trouble.

When the winter's work was finished we found we had cleared thirty-three roubles and collected well over a hundredweight of wool. We dispatched the wool by rail and decided to walk home ourselves. Anxious to keep my father's mind off the chapel, I suggested we go by the lanes and side-roads, but that was no good as everywhere was so deep in snow that we had to stick to the main road all the time. As we trudged along I plied him with the most fascinating topics of conversation that I could think of—what a fine job he had found for us that winter, how much money we had earned, hadn't we worked hard, hadn't it been a good idea of his not to spend any money on train fares but to walk home instead, and so on. By the third day I had run out of happy topics and was having to resort to sad, shared memories.

Soon after lunch that day I caught a glimpse of the chapel through the trees. Taking my father's arm I said earnestly, 'Do you remember that old nag we had—the one that stumbled under a load of brushwood and broke a leg and we had to kill it?'

'What can you do, though?' said my father, miserably. 'It's the will of God. We paid eight roubles for that horse, too. Still, it worked hard and we did get three back on the hide.'

We chattered on about our troubles and had covered

another six miles at least before father said, 'But where's this chapel, then?'

He stopped and looked around him. With the most innocent expression I could muster I replied, surprised, 'Good Lord! We must have passed it without noticing. In fact I think it's about six miles back. Well, it's hardly worth going back now, is it? It's getting late and we must put up for the night. I'll come back in the morning if you think it's really necessary, but surely God is the same everywhere, isn't he? Can't we put the money in the bowl in our own church at home?'

'All right,' said my father, grimly. 'I'll go back myself. I know you too well. You'd do anything with the money but put it in the bowl. I'll do it myself.'

Those were the last words we had on the subject. My father went back, but I never found out whether he really did light a candle to atone for my sin, or put the money back.

TWO

Youth

A day came when the hungry life began to seem to me no
life at all. To get out into the world became my one ambition.
My elder brothers worked in the town and earned no more
than ten roubles a week, out of which they had to pay board
and lodging. Moreover they were always under threat of
dismissal and of having to look for a new job. Yet my
brothers refused to return to the village. Then there was
Uncle Vasilii, my mother's brother, the manager of a big
draper's store in Verkhno-Uralsk, who earned sixty roubles
a month, and sometimes gave my mother material for a
dress or shawls. Now *there* was an enviable situation! Maybe
I would be able to get something even better in our town?

The summer of 1905 was warm with ample rains. In the
woods you could hardly move for mushrooms. A real mush-
room picker's first concern has always been to discover the
best places, and I knew one such place very well. Pepper
mushrooms and whites grew there in abundance. Of course
I kept this place a secret. You could pick two big baskets of
the very smallest mushrooms there in no time. I was often
sent to the market in the town to sell mushrooms, berries,
and dairy produce; it had been established that I was a much
better salesman than my father or mother. So one day on
my way to market I decided to seize the opportunity, and
try and find myself a job in Shuya.

Trade was pretty brisk that day and I had soon sold everything I had brought to market. I carried two bucketfuls of mushrooms which had been bought by the priest from the Spassky church to his house. On the way he asked me where I was from and how old I was and why I was trusted to come to town on my own. My answers seemed to satisfy him. Encouraged by his interest I asked him whether he knew of a suitable job for me in the town. After a little thought he said that a tradesman was looking for a boy, and took me to see him. The man was a shoe dealer, Arsenii Nikanorovich Bobkov by name. He had a shop and some workrooms, and also distributed materials for people to sew shoes at home. He looked me over from head to foot and asked suspiciously what I was doing in town without my parents. I told him the plain truth: my parents had sent me to sell mushrooms because I could get a better price than they could. The shop-keeper and the priest laughed, and the shop-keeper said 'That's just what I need.' I asked him about conditions of employment in a businesslike way and Bobkov replied: 'Something like this: you get no pay for four years, just food and clothing. Apart from that, bring your parents along and we'll talk about it.'

My father didn't want to let me go. 'I'm often ill,' he said, 'and I need someone to help here.' This worried my conscience, but early one morning I told my mother my mind was made up and then set off for Shuya, just as I was, barefoot, in my shirt and trousers, and turned up alone at the shopkeeper's house. Three days later my parents came. They tried for a long time to talk me into going back to the village. I refused point-blank and they were forced to agree.

I remember my master most of all by his nose. It was a bulbous thing, mottled fawn and red from constant drinking. I remember him also by the steady stream of swearing **and**

abuse which accompanied his every word. He was unbeliev-
ably mean. Not a day passed, as I recall, when he did not get
drunk. It was never his own money—he always drank at the
expense of those who came to him with work. He called
this 'wetting a bargain.' He had a large family: a wife, a
daughter-in-law with a child, and four other children of his
own. The eldest, Aleksandr, who was twenty, was never
rough with me, and on Sundays gave me five kopeks to clean
his shoes. The other son, eighteen-year-old Nikolai, was
unfortunately like his father.

Bobkov and his wife lived downstairs behind a screen in
the kitchen. The front half of the ground floor was let out
to tenants. My living place in the winter was in the kitchen
near the stove and in the shed in summer. I stayed here for
seven years, until I was called up for military service. I did
all kinds of things; I worked as a porter, I tended the stoves,
I brought hides from town to the warehouse, and took shoes
from the warehouse to the shop, I helped my master's wife
about the house, looked after the cow, and brought my
master his food and his vodka. After a year I began to sell in
the shop. Though small I was very strong and I took my
work at a gallop. My master never stopped cursing me, but
he seemed pleased with my work all the same.

The clothes they gave me were repulsive. They came
straight off my master's back without any alteration and in
the worst possible condition. But I shook off all these troubles,
and the thrashings, of which there were many—to me they
were just steps to my burning dream of getting out into the
world. Yet how I longed for someone to treat me like a
human being! Even at this distance of time my gratitude
goes out to Aleksandr and some of the friends who came to
see him; they always treated me well and with warmth. The
miserable surroundings gave their kindness a special glow.

One of Aleksandr's frequent visitors was a student, Rubachev, who came to town each summer for the holidays. The son of a poor civil servant, he was studying on a scholarship and lived meagrely with his widowed mother. He noticed that I often took vodka to my master. 'Oh, Sanka,' he used to say, 'in three years' time you too will have learned to drink, smoke and swear in this appalling way.' I would reply hotly: 'That will never be!' Apparently he didn't take my reply seriously for he would return to the subject whenever he came into the shop. He took a lot of trouble over my education and gave me problems to solve such as I had never been given at school. I especially liked arithmetic.

One day he said, with unusual earnestness: 'Sanka, I see that you are fond of Aleksandr and me. Give us your firm promise that you will never start drinking, and that you will never smoke and never swear.' Without thinking about it, but straight from my heart, I replied: 'I swear that I shall never, never drink, shall never swear and never smoke!'

This boyish oath played a big part in my later life. How many people have I met who have mocked me for keeping off vodka and tobacco! They called me a weakling, they called me a puritan; but their mockery remained without effect. I have even met commanders who have ordered me to drink but I have always stood my ground. And I can say more: no matter how many difficulties I have encountered in my life I have never been tempted to drown them in vodka.

The time did come, however, when I released myself from the absolute terms of my vow. In the second half of the Patriotic War, when we were beginning to score some successes, I once said that on Victory Day I would break the oath which I had sworn in 1907 and would drink before the face of all good people. And so on Victory Day, that day of tears and triumphs, I did drink four glasses of red wine to the applause and shouts of approval of my comrades-in-arms and their wives. From that day on you could, I suppose, call me a drinker, even though I still prefer mineral water and fruit juice to alcohol. But I have still to learn to smoke and swear.

I had, however, never promised Rubachev that I would not play cards. On the long winter evenings my master's wife and I—she was a great lover of cards—played 'Beggar My Neighbour.' I had to be her constant partner; I could not refuse. The master disliked our playing cards and, although we only used a small lamp, always grumbled that we were burning too much kerosene. As he went to his bed behind the partition he would sternly order us to go to bed quickly, and then would promptly fall asleep. On one occasion he awoke, came back into the kitchen, saw that it was one o'clock in the morning and that we were still fighting it out, and grew horribly angry. Spitting on his hands, as was his wont, he took a swing at me, but I nipped under the table and the blow fell on a stool instead. Barefoot and wearing only my shirt I dashed out into the cold passage, and immediately heard my master lock and bar the door. I shivered helplessly, standing barefoot on the stone floor. Presently it grew quiet again in the kitchen, my partner silently unfastened the door and I crept to my bed on the platform. My master, however, was still restless. He kept pounding on the partition, and at last shouted: 'Mother, mother, where is our lime water embrocation?' This 'lime water' was an infusion of lime buds in vodka. It was my master's favourite medicine—a panacea for all ills. Sleepily his wife replied: 'Over there . . . under the mirror . . . '

Next morning, before dawn, I went out to the yard and returned as usual with a great armful of logs, just as my master emerged from behind the partition. His whole face

was the blackest black and there were black stains in his
grey beard. I gaped, dropped the bundle of logs and fled
back to the yard. Since when did a face and beard turn black
from a bruise on the hip! It turned out that in the dark my
master had swigged a bottle of ink instead of the lime water.
He spent the next two days in the bathhouse trying to wash
it off, to the great delight of the neighbourhood.

Cards drew me into another adventure. One of my jobs
was to clean my master's shoes and those of his two sons.
For this service Aleksandr gave me five kopeks every Sunday,
but Kolka, as we called Nikolai, gave me nothing. In fact
when he discovered that I had saved up six five-kopek pieces
he decided he would take them off me, and for lack of a
better idea suggested we should play cards for money. I told
him I did not want to play—I had only thirty kopeks, and
he would beat me by sheer weight of money; moreover, I
had no cards. But Kolka had the answer to this: 'I won't
wager more than you have, and as for cards why not use
mother's?' The cards were old and I knew them well.
Reckoning that this at least gave me an equal chance, I
agreed. 'You go on up into the hayloft,' I said, 'and I'll go
and get the cards.'

But before joining him I slipped behind the woodpile and
prayed to God, as was my custom, that he might help me
win the game. In return I promised to light a candle, its
price to depend on how much I won. We played 'The Three-
Card Game.' In an hour I won twenty-eight kopeks. The
following Sunday Kolka asked me to play again, and again
I won—this time sixty kopeks. I played calmly, as I now had
some experience of playing for money and, besides, knew the
cards better than before. Kolka seemed to me to be a very

reckless player; his greed inflamed him and soon, not content with playing on Sundays, he asked me to play on weekdays as well.

Of course I sometimes lost, but comparatively rarely. When I saved up more than a rouble, I hurriedly gave the money to my mother. The first time I took her a rouble and a half. She did not want to take it and kept asking where it had come from. 'What a lot of money!' she kept on repeating. When I told her that I had won the money from Kolka, she took it with a sigh and begged me not to play any more.

Kolka was keen to win his money back. His losses already amounted to two roubles. I was afraid that he would get hold of some new cards, but he had no such intention as he too had studied our pack. So I could not attribute my successes to my knowledge of the cards, but had to put them down to the way in which I fulfilled my promise to God: if I won fifty kopeks I lit a two-kopek candle; if I won a rouble, a three-kopek candle, and if I happened to win more I bought a five-kopek candle. Kolka never learned this trick.

Wild money leads to wild ideas. Shuya was a big district town with many factories. One of the richest inhabitants was a manufacturer called Shchekoldin. It was rumoured that he owned up to four million roubles! Had he not sold all his factories in his old age? And didn't he live on the interest thereof in a house that by our standards was luxurious?

In Shuya there was a big single-storey red-brick building, the Meeting House of the gentry, in which there was a large assembly hall. Visiting artistes often gave concerts there. Twice I had managed to get in to performances without a ticket. Everybody in town knew that the eighth seat in the second row was Shchekoldin's—when he was not there himself the seat remained empty. For some reason or other I got it into my head that I would win three roubles and twenty

kopeks from Kolka. If I did, I would buy myself a ticket for
the eighth seat in the front row and sit in front of Shchekoldin
As always I gave God my promise: if all turned out well I
would light another candle. It worked.

A Ukrainian troupe was in town. To be certain of my
ticket for that eighth seat in the front row, I ran to the ticket
office long before it opened. Half an hour before the concert
was due to begin I was in the theatre.

At the first bell the common folk hurried in to take seats;
after the second bell the gentry strolled into the hall. I had
not yet made up my mind to go in. Then came the third bell.
Summoning up my courage I set off sedately towards the
door, where stood a tall, lanky usher. He seized me uncere-
moniously by the collar and thrust me back. I took my ticket
out of my pocket and showed it to my assailant. You should
have seen his face! This was probably the most difficult case
that he had ever met during his time as an usher. What was
he to do? According to the ticket he had to let me in, but
according to my clothes he had to throw me out. He muttered
something to a man who had rushed up to the scene. Then a
half made-up artiste put his head round a door and asked what
the fuss was about. Pointing at me the usher said, 'This kid has
a ticket for the front row, but look how he's dressed!' The
artiste flashed a grin at me and said: 'If you give him three
roubles and twenty kopeks back, you needn't let him in'—
and slammed the door. After a short pause the merciless
hand let go of my collar and I went to my seat.

The audience had been watching this fracas with interest
and the laughter in the hall grew louder. When I had taken
my seat I looked back at Shchekoldin. What a lad I was!
After my first backward glance the laughter grew louder, and
when I looked round a second time almost everybody was
roaring. Many of the people at the back stood up to get a

better look at what was making the people at the front laugh. As I sauntered around in the foyer during the interval many people came up to me, and they all asked me the same question: 'Who bought your ticket for you?' Apparently they thought that one of the rich townsfolk had wished to poke fun at Shchekoldin. Some of them tweaked my ear with a laugh and said approvingly: 'Well, what a daredevil!' Suddenly Aleksandr, my master's son, who was strolling past with a girl, saw me. He walked quickly up to me and asked me in some alarm where I had got the money. Calmly looking him straight in the eye, I replied: 'I won it off Kolka.' His mind set at rest he laughed, took his lady's arm and went off. In the second and third acts, to my great disappointment, the seat behind me was empty. Shchekoldin had preferred to leave.

On the following day there was a lot of talk in town about the events at the assembly hall. The rumour reached my master. He was sitting in a pub when a merchant said to him, 'Arsenii Nikanorovich, your lad has been robbing you.'

'No, that can't be. He's an honest lad.'

'But do you know that on Saturday he was at the assembly hall and sat in the front row? Those tickets cost more than three roubles. He was even sitting in front of Shchekoldin.'

My master, greatly dismayed, hurried to the shop. Blocking the door with his carcass he yelled at me: 'Where did you get the money for the ticket, you sonofabitch?' Without a moment's thought I replied that I had won the money at cards from Kolka. Rolling up his sleeves my master spat on his hands like a real boxer and landed two painful blows on me with his fist. Of course I did not wait for the next instalment but slipped out between him and the wall, and that was that. He beat Kolka three days running, despite the fact that his son was already the same size as himself.

It probably seems strange that I should remember such small day-to-day incidents in those years when events of enormous importance were taking place in Russia—the first Russian revolution—and even in Shuya, where there was a strong working-class movement and where 'Comrade Arsenii'—Mikhail Vasilevich Frunze—was operating.

And yet is it so strange? I lived in such surroundings, and I was so bound up with the shop and my master's house that the range of my impressions and interests was almost entirely confined to their limits, the more so because my extremely pious and patriarchal family background had taught me to live from day to day concentrating on my work, my pay, and how to maintain a barely tolerable existence.

My elder brothers, who worked in a factory, were in my eyes and in those of my parents simply people who had found themselves another way of earning their living outside the village; the fact that their new membership of the working class had changed their ideas and their attitude towards the world could hardly be guessed at even by my father and mother, let alone myself who was still, remember, a mere child. As I see no merit in showing myself other than I was then, I shall stick to telling what really filled my life during these years.

I should say that I first heard about 'Comrade Arsenii' in 1907—I well remember the anger of the workers at his arrest. The authorities considered him to be the organiser of all strikes in the region of Ivanovo and Shuya and promised, so it was said, a reward of ten thousand roubles to anyone who would deliver him up alive or dead. Although the workers tried hard to protect Arsenii, an informer managed to nose out the place where he was staying and report it to the police. Arsenii was arrested and imprisoned in Shuya jail. The news spread quickly, not only in Shuya but in other nearby towns and factories, and the workers moved into the town by whatever means they could find. On the following day Shuya was flooded with workers. A battalion of infantry called from Vladimir appeared in the town, and the jail was ringed by troops. The factories came out on strike, shops closed and normal life stopped. Then a rumour started that Arsenii had written a message to all the assembled workers and handed it to a delegation of them, asking them to take no action so as to avoid all bloodshed, though he thanked them warmly for their comradely solidarity. Next day Arsenii was taken under strong escort to the prison in Vladimir. In Shuya there began a round of general searches and arrests which continued for three weeks.

One day I saw my brother Nikolai standing outside the window of the shop where I worked. I went out to him. Nikolai told me that he had to flee in order to avoid arrest. He was leaving his wife and child in the village for the time being, but would come back for them at the first opportunity. He asked me to give his greetings to my parents and to all our relatives. When I asked him how much money he had, it turned out to be only twenty kopeks. Unfortunately I too only had sixty kopeks. I wanted to borrow some more from Aleksandr, but my brother would not allow it. We parted after a warm embrace. I did not know that this was the last time I would see him. It was not until two years later that his wife and child joined him in Siberia, where he had started work on the Olovyannaya Station. He was called up into the army in 1915 and was shot at Brest for inciting the men travelling with him to the front to mutiny. My parents learned of this through a letter from a soldier who would not give his name.

After working for my master for three years I knew the shoe business quite as well as any of his other apprentices. Customers came to me rather than to the other salesmen, probably thinking that it would be easier to squeeze a good bargain out of a boy; but the experience I had gained on my mitten-selling journeys helped me, and I could get a better price for any pair of shoes than the boss himself.

I had grown a great deal over the last six months and now, considering myself an adult, I decided to ask my master to start giving me a wage a year early. He showed no surprise and merely asked: 'How much do you want?' 'A hundred roubles a year,' I replied firmly, 'with board and clothes supplied by you as before.' Moreover I insisted that I should not have to carry laundry through the town to the river, and that my master should not beat me. Finally we agreed that for the coming year, 1908, I would receive sixty roubles and the following year a hundred. My other conditions were accepted.

THREE

First Love

By the time I had worked in the shoe trade for five years I had become a first-class salesman. One day a girl came into the shop. She was not very tall, but she was pretty and demure. She chose some shoes for herself, quietly said good-bye and went out. I very much wanted to see her again, even if only at a distance. My wish was granted: she came into the shop again to buy rubbers for the heels. As I was wrapping her purchase up I summoned up my courage and suggested that she should bring the shoes in and I would fix the rubbers. She thanked me but refused. Soon, however, she was back again with the shoes and asked me to fasten the rubbers on for her. I tried as hard as I could to make her visit to the shop last longer by working as slowly as possible. She sat attentively and watched my work. Neither of us said a single word.

I had a friend called Lenka, who worked in the shop opposite ours. He was a year younger than I but much more dashing with the girls. On working days he and I went for walks together but on Sunday Lenka would go off with the girls and I wandered about on my own. One summer's day I came across Lenka with two girls in the park, one of them the customer I had liked so much. How I cursed the stupid timidity that stopped me from going up to them and walking with them!

We would probably never have got to know each other

if I had not met Lenka again on the following Sunday, with the same two girls. He came up to me to tell me that one of the girls wanted to make my acquaintance. I started to refuse but it wasn't as easy as all that to get rid of Lenka. He persuaded me, accused me of discourtesy and maintained that this acquaintance laid no obligation on me. 'If you don't like her,' he said, 'all you need to do is just pass the time of day with her.'

The two girls came across to us and Lenka said: 'That's her.' It was my customer. Her name was Olya and her friend was called Vera. Lenka and Vera soon went away, and Olya and I were left alone. We sat down on a bench and said nothing. Her first words were: 'It's very late—it's time I was going home.' We walked quietly towards her house, still silent. Before we got to the house Olya gave me her hand and we parted. I was sure she had noticed the happiness in my eyes as I looked at her.

Four months went by from the date of our first meeting. Each Sunday I met her in the park but she was always with her girl friends. We exchanged greetings from afar. I could never make up my mind to go up to her.

Lenka once told me that Olya was studying to become a dressmaker and lived with her parents and two brothers. Some time later he told me that Olya had shown surprise at my constant lonely walks and could not understand why I did not go and talk to her. I was forced to admit that my only excuse was that she was always with other girls. So the following Sunday I found Olya by herself. I quickly walked up to her and we set off together. We sat down on a bench for three hours and never said a word. We parted happy and sad. These silent meetings went on for more than two years. During all that time it was looks alone that deepened our mutual attraction.

Once, in September, 1912, we met in the main street. Olya seemed agitated. As it grew dark she said softly: 'Shura, I must talk to you. Let's slip down a side lane.' My heart almost died of happiness: had Olya suddenly decided to be the first to put into words what we both had felt? But it took her all her strength to whisper: 'They are marrying me to Peter.' I do not know how I managed to say it: 'I know him. He will make a good husband, a good father. Marry him.' Olya burst into tears. She reproached me: 'Why praise him to me? You know that I only love you.' At this I too burst into tears; I told her that I loved her just as strongly, but lacked words for my love. 'Shura, why are we waiting?' she whispered through her tears. 'If we love each other why do you advise me to marry someone else?' How could I conceal my grief? I told her that in three weeks I would be drafted into the army for three or four years. How could I marry her to leave her neither a wife nor a widow? There was also much serious talk of war. 'That is why I am telling you to get married.' Olya again burst into bitter tears. For a long time we walked along the dark lanes and for the first time we talked without shame of the feelings we had kept pent up within us for two and a half years. Olya thanked me for my true and pure love. We parted, still in tears.

Three weeks later I was called up. On that very day Olya was married. She had invited me to her wedding, just to see me for one last time. I did not go.

Part Two

FOUR

A Tsarist Soldier and the Revolution

In October, 1912, after squaring accounts with my employer, I went back to my village to say goodbye to my parents. Then, together with other conscripts, I went to Orel and was drafted to the 17th Chernigovskii Hussars. They said the hardest service was in the infantry and the longest in the navy, so I was very glad to join the cavalry. The cavalrymen, however, told me that theirs was indeed the most arduous service of all: an infantryman only had his rifle, but a cavalryman had a sabre, a lance, a horse and a saddle, all of which he must learn to use and all of which he must look after, and the horse above all the rest. Looking after a horse took five hours a day and more, then there were still the periods of instruction to be put in. The only thing that made life easier for a cavalryman was not having to footslog on the march; but some of the horses could give your guts such a shaking that footslogging might have been better after all.

But to me cavalry service did not seem difficult. Military knowledge came easily and I was reckoned a good soldier. At first I got one of those stubborn mounts which will not walk but only jogs about at the trot, and shies at fences and the cane-splitting stands in sabre practice—in other words, a horse from which I could expect all kinds of unpleasantness all the time. But soon it was replaced by another mount which came up to the jump fences confidently and was quite steady during cane-splitting. Its name was Amulet and it greatly helped me to become a good rider.

Every squadron had its singers but our squadron's, the 6th's, were considered the best and were often called to the officers' mess at night, to entertain the drunken officers. I was one of the singers. Often we were given two-kopek rolls as a reward. The lion's share of these went to our sergeant-of-horse, Shcherbak.

The rich fighting history of our regiment went back to the eighteenth century. In 1910 it was under the command of the Tsar's brother, the Grand Duke Mikhail Alexandrovich. His great strength had become a legend. It was commemorated in the officers' mess by a glass case containing a silver dish rolled into a tube and a pack of cards torn in two from side to side. The independent cavalry brigade of which our regiment formed part was under the command of Major General Abram Dragomirov, the son of the famous General Dragomirov.

Our squadron's recruits were under the care of Staff Captain Sviderskii. He was tall and broad-shouldered, and alarmingly strong. He knew his job and was never late on parade, but he was exceptionally severe and a fault-picker to an unbelievable degree. He would beat a soldier ferociously with all his strength for the slightest inaccuracy or shortcoming. He struck me once—a blow on the leg just above the knee with the flat of his sabre blade. I carried the weal for a long time. Sviderskii left us as a lieutenant-colonel in 1915. I happened to meet him again in 1925 in quite different circumstances, a meeting which I shall describe later.

Although we had very little free time we, the men, still found time for friendly gossip, to share memories and discuss the officers. Looking back, it strikes me that the men's assessment of the officers was very accurate, although half the troopers were completely illiterate.

The men had almost no contact with the officers, but we used to chat with their orderlies and from them often heard what our masters were talking about. It was in this way that we learned that Russia would probably soon be going to war, and we all awaited this with fear.

Then war was declared.

Our regiment, under the command of Colonel Blokhin, was concentrated in the region of Kholm (now Chelm, in Poland). We were joined by uhlan and dragoon regiments to form the 17th Cavalry Division. General Dragomirov took command. We were to fight in the Carpathian Mountains.

After our first few successful actions Colonel Blokhin was promoted to general and become our brigade commander. Colonel Dessius was appointed to command us in his place. He was a tall, hefty man of fifty-five with stooping shoulders and grey temples. We liked him, but the officers did not. Which of us was right, the men or the officers? I shall give you some facts characteristic of him and you can judge.

Once four horses in our squadron were killed by a shell. They were buried. After the regiment had moved forward another thirty-five miles our squadron commander, in a written report, asked the colonel's permission to cross off these horses from the regimental lists. Back came the reply: 'Exhume the horses, skin them and they may then be taken off the lists on presentation of a receipt for the sale of the hides.' A party of three troopers, myself in charge, was sent to carry out the order. The horses had been buried seven days before, but we did as we were told and the horses were duly taken off the lists.

Another time the regimental commander was informed by the veterinary surgeon that the backs of many of the officers' pack horses were raw. He immediately ordered that packs should weigh no more than one hundredweight (two trunks on the sides and a bedroll on top). Any officer who disobeyed this order would be severely punished. Any excess weight would be taken off and destroyed. About a week later, in the morning, after we had broken camp, the regiment was drawn up near a village and all pack horses were brought forward and unloaded. Scales were brought out and weighing began. An excess of ten pounds over the limit was allowed. The orderlies could chose what was to be removed from overweight packs. Kerosene was poured over the resulting heap and it was set on fire.

One day, after a night in camp, the regiment was paraded and the regimental commander said to the troopers: 'Lads, I have heard a rumour that you are being badly fed, in other words, cheated. In your presence I draw the attention of all officers to the fact that they are to pay greater attention to the food for their men and to the performance of their quartermasters. And to you, lads, my order is: if you get less than three ounces as your portion of meat, bring it to me direct, by-passing your immediate commanders.' After this, our food improved a great deal.

Let me give you one last example of our colonel's ways. As there was nothing to feed the horses on in the hills they were sent about a hundred and twenty miles down into the valley, while we, dismounted, stayed behind to defend the Dukla Pass. But the Germans broke through the defences on our right, near the town of Tarnow, and drove back our forces towards the east. Presently we also received the order to withdraw. Early next morning the regimental commander assembled the regiment and said to us: 'Lads, the Germans have broken through the front to our right. We are threatened with encirclement, prison camp and destruction. We shall have to cover about one hundred and twenty miles on foot in three days. If we can do it, we shall preserve the flag which our regiment has carried with honour for more than a hundred years, and we shall save our lives. The officers have horses but they are not to mount, and neither will I. I will march at the head of the regiment all the way although I am older than you are by many years. Thirty or forty miles a day is no rarity for our glorious infantry. Are we any worse than they? What's your answer, lads?' As one man the whole regiment roared out: 'Let's go!' That made the colonel glow with pleasure. We set off and, true enough, the regimental commander marched in front all the way, leaning on a great stick like a shepherd's crook. At each halt the squadrons changed places, the rear squadrons coming up to the front, because it is always easier to march in the lead.

Towards the end of the first day some officers, among them the Andreev brothers, sons of the governor of Orel province, left the ranks and to our laughter and jeers climbed into the carts. By the end of the third day half the officers had got into carts and two-wheeled trucks, as there was no more room in the ambulance wagons. But despite their great weariness the men kept up their spirits. They rose still higher when we saw our horses waiting for us in the valley.

Our regiment was reckoned the best fighting force in the division, particularly at the beginning of the war. One particular attack against enemy cavalry comes to my mind. With my lance at the tilt I charged an enemy trooper who was riding towards me. My lance pierced him with such force that I could hardly keep my seat in the saddle. There was no time to think of freeing the lance. Indeed time, not I, was the master then, carrying me forward like a thunderbolt in a tempest. I drew my sabre and cut down two more of the enemy.

The men of the Chernigov Regiment also fought well on foot. But I remember one incident to the regiment's shame. During the general retreat from Galicia the cavalry were covering the withdrawal of our troops, often fighting dismounted. On one such occasion we beat back four attacks. When the fifth attack came it was designed to overawe us with waves of men in close formation supported by columns of companies. The regiment broke and fell back, leaving in the trenches only two Maxim machine-guns and their crews with two senior N.C.O.s. These alone drove back the attack. When the regiment returned to its former position, it was ashamed of itself.

The two heroic N.C.O.s each received the St. George's Cross, First Class, and were promoted to ensign, the most junior officer rank. But to our general surprise they were suddenly posted to a regiment of uhlans: the officers and gentlemen of our regiment did not wish to shake hands with former 'rankers.' Not all the officers in our regiment were like this, but for the majority caste and professional privilege were what counted most. Needless to say officers of this kind were of no help in upholding the men's morale, which was already suffering under the horrors of war.

When we were attacking in 1914 we won victory after victory, and at that time even large losses did not depress the men. But when the general retreat began—when, without a fight, we abandoned ground that we had won with our blood—dejection became more and more pronounced and malicious remarks about the High Command became frequent among the men. The reinforcements which reached us from the depths of the country increased our feeling of depression, with their talk of coming famine and of the incapacity of our rulers. The troops also found it hard to bear the neglect by the officers of the men's most urgent needs. Often it happened that when we came to a village where we were to stay the night nothing was ready; we would have to stand around and wait, mortally tired all of us, until the allocation of billets had been sorted out. And it might happen that when the horses had been unsaddled, and the troopers had fetched supper in their mess-tins, the order suddenly rang out: 'Saddle up!' It would turn out that we must go to another street, or to another village even, because the place where we had been told to stop was allocated to others. It was at times like this that our officers got their full share of bitter remarks and curses.

Of course all this contributed to a falling-off in discipline which was most noticeable when we went on the defensive after a prolonged withdrawal. The men lost heart and began to consider the enemy unbeatable. They had no faith in the strength of their positions and looked on them as merely a delay on the road to further retreat. I saw all this and stored it all in my memory, and it made me think.

When I look back I feel sure that, despite all the troubles which I suffered in my childhood and early youth, there was still much of the child in me, right up to the time when I joined the army. My first real manly action, I think, was to reject of my own free will the girl I loved, so as not to make her unhappy. Let this not seem an exaggeration. It was this action that helped me to grow up in mind, and enter army life with sufficient maturity to turn my natural bent for involvement in any risky business into the well calculated gambling that is the very life of a front-line soldier. What also helped me was the habit of prudent calculation I had had since childhood.

Many of my comrades in the regiment, when they first met war, were afraid—afraid of being wounded and left on the field of battle, afraid of being killed and buried in

foreign soil—and so they came to dread their encounters with
the enemy. As far as I can remember I felt no such fear.
Incidentally, I discovered at the front that no trace now
remained of my former piety. It had been grafted into me
as a child, it had hung on as a formality, by force of habit,
as it were, into the early years of my youth, but while many
men previously indifferent to religion began partly to trust
in God, I on the contrary became convinced that all strength
comes from man himself, from his mind and will. So that
when we were not at grips with the enemy I even felt slightly
disappointed, and always preferred to be on patrol or in the
leading detachment rather than swallowing dust as we
jogged along on the march. My superiors valued my constant
readiness to go off on reconnaissance but, to do them justice,
they never took advantage of it; on the contrary, they very
often restrained me.

I have already said that the war taught me to think
seriously about what I had seen and experienced. Ideas
about politics, however, came to me only later, under the
direct impact of the Revolution; until then I was almost
entirely taken up with thoughts about my everyday military
duties, and those duties were by no means light.

So many interesting things happened to me between 1914
and 1917 that I could never tell about them all. But I will
try to tell at least something.

Once, for example, I was put in charge of a patrol to carry
out a reconnaissance. We advanced along a road lined with
tall lime trees towards a large village, making our approach
with all due care. Two of our troopers inspected a house
standing on its own and gave a sign that it was free of the
enemy. By an agreed signal I ordered them to go on to the
village to investigate the outlying houses while I and the

rest of my men rode quickly to the house they had cleared.
I dismounted, told the men to keep a careful watch all round
outside and, hitching the reins over the fence, I hurried into
the house. Hardly was I over the threshold when two shots
rang out and I heard shouting outside. I rushed out just in
time to see my patrol, including the two troopers, tearing
off down the road under enemy fire. I jumped into the
saddle and galloped after them. I had barely got three
hundred yards from the house when bullets began to whistle
past me. One of them wounded my horse. It stumbled and
fell. It seemed a pity to leave the enemy my saddle but I
could already see enemy infantrymen hurrying after me. I
had no choice but to run to a nearby ditch and make my way
back along it. When they saw my fallen horse the enemy,
for some reason, stopped chasing me. They also lost track of
my patrol.

My way lay over a small river, with a bridge across it.
I set off towards it but then saw an enemy patrol approaching
the bridge from the other side. My main worry was to make
sure that the enemy did not spot me. I looked around. Not
far from the bridge there was a big, plump willow tree over-
hanging the water and I decided I would be safer under it
than under the bridge, since by peering between the branches
I would get a clear sight of the approaching enemy, while I
myself remained hidden from them. I crawled along the
steep bank to the willow tree and settled down with my rifle
at the ready. Soon the enemy patrol could be heard
approaching. They drew level with the tree and went past.
When they had got some fifty paces away from me I sent
five shots after them, reloaded quickly and began to fire
again. The patrol galloped away leaving two wounded men
lying on the road.

It occurred to me then that on the range I could put

thirty-eight shots out of forty into the target, yet here, firing at big objects over a short distance, the best I could show was two out of five.

On another occasion, we had reached a small town near the Dukla Pass and were given a free afternoon. Our squadron was not due to move into its defensive area until the next day. The town was surrounded by high hills and I wanted to climb one of them in order to look over the area. Up till then I had never climbed hills like this one and I misjudged the time I would need. The hill proved to be thickly wooded and it took me some time to reach the summit.

When I looked around I was struck by a kind of beauty I had never seen before. Below me at the foot of the mountain lay the village, and curling away from it behind a hill the road along which we had travelled. All round me the mountains rose higher still, particularly towards the enemy, from where I could hear shots. In front of me stretched a great plateau. 'I must go and have a look at it,' I decided. When I had walked about half a mile I found myself among some trenches which had recently been occupied by our troops. The trenches were shallow and their walls were crumbling. I was particularly struck by the large number of cartridge cases which were lying about and the great heaps of them where machine-guns must have stood. There were spades, ammunition sacks and bloodstained uniforms all over the place. I saw many graves, not one of them marked by an inscription or even by a stake. The sight of the carelessly buried corpses was very depressing. Here and there a shoulder showed above the ground; bare feet, legs and arms stuck out at odd angles and sometimes you could see a face. I wanted to look at the trenches from which the enemy, during the recent fighting, had kept our troops under fire. When I got to them they also impressed me, but for a very different reason: these trenches were deep and their walls and floors were lined with twigs. They were absolutely clean and there was not a sign of military litter, not even cartridge cases. In a big German cemetery in the valley, to which I went down, every grave had been carefully dug and every grave was marked by a cross with an inscription about the man they had buried there.

I was absorbed in my thoughts and entirely failed to notice that the sun had set. In the quickly gathering dusk I felt suddenly an inexplicable terror. I quickened my step and began to sing loudly, trying to overcome the great feeling of desolation which was creeping into my heart. When I finally reached the path I began to run. I ran headlong as I had done once when I was a boy, and had gone into the forest to look for the fern flower and met the incomprehensible life of the night, face to face.

Another episode of the war comes back to me. We were holding a position to the north of Lutski, beyond the river Styr, and shared a marsh over a mile across with the enemy. A cavalry division needs a lot of hay. In this place it was difficult both to buy and to deliver it. This suited the quartermaster sergeant and certain officers very well; they made a very tidy profit out of it. Only our friend the horse could not make out why his daily ration had shrunk so greatly, and the horses looked at us most reproachfully. The marsh, however, was full of haystacks. The hay was of poor quality, but in those days even sedge was reckoned good fodder. At first we took the hay from the nearest stacks. Then we had to venture out to the middle of the marsh and take hay from stacks farther off, without stopping even for machine-gun fire. By the second half of the winter we were taking hay from stacks right up close to the enemy lines, and despite all our precautions one of our men was taken prisoner. These sorties, although extremely risky, were essential. One could not bear to look at the starving horses, which had already eaten all the rotting straw from the thatches. Out foraging for straw we also noticed there were cranberries growing on the hummocks. We set about clearing the nearby hummocks and moved out to those in the middle of the marsh. Enemy machine-gun fire forced us to crawl but we went on collecting the berries in spite of it.

The officers turned a blind eye to our risky hay-gathering operations, which suited them well, because they reckoned that they could pass off the hay we had collected as hay they had bought. They severely forbade the picking of cranberries. But our berry-picking jaunts continued. Soldiers have a sweet tooth! Or, more to the point perhaps, everyone gets bored of eating out of the common pot and wants something fresh and tasty. This craving is sometimes so strong that it drives men to take risks that are not justified by any serious standard.

In 1915, when we were leaving the Carpathians, we had only five or ten rounds each, and there were almost no shells left at all. The Germans who were pursuing us stopped at the outskirts of a wood. There was about a thousand yards between the opposing forces. At the edge of the wood we could make out a small forester's hut with a straw thatch; there was one window facing us, another on the side, and we could not see the door. All of us were sure that the hut was being used by the Germans. Thirsting for strong sensations our officers announced: 'Whoever can put a match to the roof of that hut will get the St. George's Cross.' My friend Sergei and I said that we would like to try. We wanted to do it at night, but the officers insisted that although we might get to the house under cover of darkness we must only set fire to it at dawn. They wanted to watch without losing any of their sleep.

An hour before dawn we were crouching by the enemy's wire. When it began to grow light, two Germans got up from a foxhole behind a bush about a hundred yards away and disappeared into the wood. We thought this must be a secret look-out over the wire at night; during the day the wire would most probably be under observation from the edge of the wood. This made us extremely careful. Our slightest blunder would be noticed by the enemy. So we crawled towards our target, using the high grass and the roughness of the ground as cover. We cut the lowest strand of wire and crawled through towards the side of the house which had no window. We halted about fifty paces from it. Sergei stayed put with his rifle at the ready to cover me in case of sudden danger, and I crawled on to the house. I was just on the point of raising a lighted match to the thatched roof when the door opened and a German came out. Sergei immediately fired at him. With a shout the German sprang back into the house and slammed the door behind him. At the same time my match went out. Our task unfinished we ran back, dodging behind the bushes, and crawled through the gap in the wire. Some shots rang out from the wood and a few men burst shouting from the house and opened fire raggedly in our direction. But we were already beyond the wire and by using the terrain to the best advantage we got back to our own people.

The officers and men of the squadron had all been watching our raid. Many of them had seen me go up to the house, and seen us both running back and falling into the bushes. All of course had heard the firing and therefore reckoned we were dead. The men were cursing the officers for making us set fire to the house at dawn, rather than at night. Everyone was surprised and delighted at our safe return, but instead of the St. George's Crosses which we had been promised we were given medals.

One final reminiscence: on another occasion, after taking our turn at sitting in the trenches, we had been relieved and had gone back to rest in the woods about thirty miles from Stokhod. One day I collected the men's meat rations and found that on average they weighed three ounces instead of the regulation four. I remembered our regimental commander's order that if this happened we should go to him direct. When I reported to the colonel he asked me what squadron I was in and whether I had weighed the rations carefully. Then he told me to go and promised to take the necessary action. As soon as I left him I began to have doubts about what I had done. I now felt that it might have been better to have taken the rations to my squadron commander. These pangs of conscience grew even stronger as I realised that it was not in fact the squadron commander who was at fault but the quartermaster sergeant.

The following day I was summoned by my squadron commander. I felt ashamed to go in. He was sitting at a table that we had made for him and was smoking a cigarette. He made me sit down and after a long silence asked me reproachfully, 'Gorbatov, why did you go to the regimental commander? Why didn't you bring the rations to me? Surely the men don't think that I make use of their ounces of meat?'

'No, we don't, but those were the C.O.'s orders,' I replied.

He looked at me steadily and offered me a cigarette, then checked himself.

'Oh no, you don't smoke or drink, do you? But you do play cards for money, and you don't often lose, so you can't be going hungry! You're a good soldier, Gorbatov. But you could be even better if you spent less time telling people how to put the world to rights and thought a bit more about yourself. You could have had four St. George's Crosses already that way. Just you drop this habit—it will bring you no good. But I can see you are already regretting what you did. Right?'

I went out as red as a lobster. The stern Staff Captain Saburov had more justice in him than the other squadron commanders put together.

At the time of the February Revolution we were at Stokhod. We, the men, knew nothing as yet but only saw that the officers were bewildered for some reason. They kept going to see one another, and gathered in small groups to discuss something with great heat. What had happened?

The orderlies sometimes managed to catch a few odd words: 'Everything's rotten, everything's corrupt, we should have expected it,' 'Worthless rulers,' 'On the brink of the precipice,' and so on. The orderlies told us about anything of this kind straight away. Official quarters kept mum but the grape-vine worked. Soon we learned of the abdication of the Tsar. We were interested to see how the officers would react to this and, through the orderlies, we tried to find out what they were thinking. In the ranks most of us thought: 'Now that we are rid of the Tsar we will probably soon be rid of the war.' Only a few were worried and asked how we would survive without a Tsar.

Quite soon those among us who knew something of politics and could understand what was going on found themselves much in demand. They tried to explain events to the other men. Until then I had had no inkling that we had some revolutionaries in the regiment. They had probably never bothered to talk to me because they could see that I was entirely wrapped up in my work as a front-line soldier. They had assumed I was not interested in politics.

We were only told officially about Tsar Nicholas II's abdication several days after the event. Our officers were probably 'awaiting instructions from above.' As we were in the front line the statement was read to us by squadrons. After Squadron Commander Saburov, by now Lieutenant-Colonel, had read the document to us he told us in a voice that, for him, was oddly tender that our duties remained the same, and that the army must continue to obey the orders of the Government and the men those of their officers. Our task was to carry the war to a victorious conclusion.

And so things went on for a time, and we fought as before. But the 'victorious conclusion' seemed to recede into the far distance; we could see no sign of it. On the contrary, soon after the February Revolution tragedy came on the Stokhod.

Our cavalry division was in position on the eastern bank of this river. It was said that its name, which means 'The Hundred Ways,' came to it because as it flowed along its broad marshy valley it had split into a multitude of small channels. In autumn, 1916, an operation was carried out immediately to our left to establish a bridgehead on the western bank, and at a great cost a narrow strip of ground was won. It was held by a rifle corps of three divisions, of which two were in the bridgehead and the third on the eastern bank. Our artillery was almost entirely deployed in the bridgehead. Three roads were laid across the river valley, over an enormous number of bridges.

The German Command were afraid that in the spring of 1917 we would attack from this bridgehead. They decided to liquidate it at the first opportunity. Our Command knew that the Germans were preparing such an operation but not when they intended to carry it out. Then the spring floods put the whole valley under water and our troops waited in great anxiety.

One dark night, on March 24th, I think it was, a German soldier, by origin a Frenchman from Alsace-Lorraine, deserted to our lines in the bridgehead. He reported that the Germans would attack in the morning. A great mass of artillery had been assembled and many poison gas containers brought up from the rear. Later we learned that throughout that night our commanders had hesitated whether to believe the deserter and move the third division into the bridgehead to strengthen it, or to withdraw the other two divisions from it. Finally they decided to move the third division across the river and to hold the bridgehead with all the means at their disposal.

The third division of the corps was transferred to the bridgehead before dawn, and at dawn a bombardment began the like of which we had never heard before. Everything came under fire simultaneously—our trenches, the bridges, the artillery, including the guns deployed on the eastern bank of the Stokhod. Soon all the bridges, most of which were clearly visible to the enemy, were destroyed. Towards the end of the bombardment the enemy released three successive waves of poison gas, the wind favouring the Germans. The gas was followed by waves of infantry in close formation.

Our troops had been warned in advance of the attack and they were able to take shelter from the artillery barrage. They used their anti-gas precautions in time, and they completely threw back the enemy with comparatively light losses to themselves. But after a brief pause the artillery opened up again, followed by gas and then another infantry charge. This time the enemy managed to drive a small gap in our defences and overran the first line of trenches. The

Germans again suffered heavy losses, but the losses among our divisions from the artillery bombardment were even heavier as their shelters had been very largely destroyed. When, after a third artillery bombardment, the Germans brought in fresh troops our infantry in the bridgehead could no longer put up any resistance. Yet it was impossible to withdraw troops across the flooded river valley. We lost both the bridgehead and three divisions.

One does not need to be skilled in military matters to understand what a bad decision our commanders had made. The men realised this and grew angry. For me personally, the tragedy on the River Stokhod served as an important lesson in later years, when I myself had to make decisions in battle.

If at one time only a very small circle had known that Private Muravev was a member of the Bolshevik party, he now made no secret of it. We often asked him to explain who were the Bolsheviks, and why they were so called. It was from him that I first heard of Lenin.

By saying that his mother was ill and making much of difficulties at home Muravev managed to get a week's leave from the squadron commander. In fact he went to Petrograd, to find out what was going on. When he came back Muravev told us that unbelievable things were happening in Petrograd, that there were in effect two authorities—that of the bourgeois Provisional Government and that of the Soviets of Workers in which Lenin's supporters had the greatest influence. This could not go on for long and it seemed likely that the bourgeois government would fall. I shall not talk about the events of those months because I have nothing to add to what the reader already knows from many other sources.

At the end of October, for reasons unknown to the men, our division was transported to the area of Narva. There were various rumours about our move to this area: some said that we had been sent there to fight against 'Bolshevik sedition' in Petrograd, others said that we were to defend Petrograd against a possible attack by the German army in Estonia.

It was here that our division first held an election for officers: a lieutenant was elected regimental commander in place of the colonel, and instead of the lieutenant-colonel a cornet was appointed squadron commander. I too was elected to the regimental committee, probably more on account of my good fighting and comradely reputation. I was no more than average in terms of political awareness, although of course an interest in social problems had already been awakened in me.

It so happened that our division did not take part in the first battles to put the Soviets into power, nor in the struggle with the German army which was trying to destroy the Red Guard.

Our regiment was transferred to the area of Volosovo Station and was billeted in nearby villages. We knew that, with the creation of a new kind of army, the old army would be demobilised. We also knew that somehow or other the men who were tired of war and worried by the difficult material situation of their families would get themselves home without waiting to be demobilised.

FIVE

The Civil War

On March 15th, 1918, we were informed that our division was to be disbanded and all its personnel demobilised. Only a soldier who has lived through a war from its very first day can understand our jubilation. We were alive! We were going home! My way home lay through Gatchina, Petrograd and Moscow. I had never seen Petrograd in peacetime. The streets had been cleared of snow only where absolutely necessary. Improvised stove-pipes poked out of windows. In the evenings the town was badly lit. Long queues for bread formed outside the bakers' shops before dawn. Yet the town seemed charged with energy.

After five and a half years' absence I returned to Shuya, my home town, on March 25th. The news that two of my brothers had died at the front cast gloom over the meeting with my parents. They had aged greatly. They were distraught: they had nothing with which to welcome me except potatoes. I told them not to worry, I had brought my billeting token. Untying my bundles, I took out seven pounds of lard, four pounds of bread and five pounds of sugar; that was the whole of what I had received when we had shared out the regimental stores. It all went to my mother. Then I undid my kitbag and shook out more gifts—rolls of cotton print for my mother and sisters. Only my father and younger brother got nothing, but my brother pointed out that he had had a present from me long ago: he was wearing the clothes and shoes which I had left behind when I went off to the army.

The morning after my return home I took a look at our house. The house and outbuildings had been in need of repair when I left; now they were ruinous. My father was old and my younger brother still an indifferent workman, and so the whole burden of looking after things fell on me. What worried me most of all was that spring was approaching and we had no seeds to sow, except for potatoes. Grain was hard to come by. Besides, we lacked the money to buy it; prices were steep.

Father told me that the neighbours had travelled to Kazan province and brought back grain bartered for cotton. When my mother and sister heard this they immediately offered to give up all that I had brought them. But I would have none of this; there was not nearly enough for the purpose anyway. I still had a little money left and bought some cotton myself. Two weeks later I returned from Kazan with grain for sowing and for grinding into flour. My front-line soldier's demobilisation card was a help on the journey. Thanks to that I not only travelled without paying, but managed to save my load; at that time guard detachments were patrolling the roads to prevent speculation and were confiscating such loads.

When we had finished sowing we decided to repair our ramshackle house. We did not have to pay for the timber we used, and our neighbours helped us to fetch it. We had a bad time underpinning the house with new timber foundations but once again there was no lack of good people around us with willing hands.

The village regarded me as an educated man who had seen something of the world and so elected me a member of the District Executive Committee and the District Committee of Poor Peasants. I took my work seriously and felt responsible for my fellow villagers, who expected me to help them in some way. They were always coming to me with the sort of questions that troubled people at that time: who were these men who had gone as far as overthrowing the Tsar? Why two revolutions? Wasn't one enough to give them their land? All of them were interested in Lenin—his life, his work and his ideas about the future. I told them all I knew. I now realise how rudimentary some of my answers were, how often I told them what should be rather than what was really happening. In those days the world-wide victory of Socialism seemed close; people would surely soon understand where the truth lay, and the end would come for the lords and masters.

But then the flames of civil war engulfed the country and it turned out that I was one of those who must defend the people's newly-won power. My mind was made up when I heard that the Party and the Government had appealed to the workers and peasants, calling for troops to fight Denikin and continue the offensive in the Urals and in Siberia.

My mother wept. She had lost two sons already. Let those who had not yet smelled gunpowder fight. As my sisters tried to comfort her they wept even more bitterly than she. My father was ill. He lay silent on a bench, just sighing deeply every now and again. At last he said, 'Stop crying. Sanka fought for four years and nothing happened to him. With God's help nothing will happen this time. We have almost repaired the house. Mikhail is a big lad now. Don't upset Sanka—it's hard enough for him as it is.' Then, turning to me: 'You have done right, son. Who will defend the Soviet power if we don't?' After this he fell silent again. I took leave of my relatives and friends and set off for the military registration office in Shuya.

I served as a private in the Red Army from 1919. Later I

commanded a troop, then a squadron, and already by 1920, in the fighting against the Poles, a regiment and the Bashkir Cavalry Brigade. There was a saying in the Tsarist Army: 'He's a bad private who doesn't see himself a general.' After the Revolution this became a real possibility in the Red Army, not just a dream.

Unfortunately I kept no diary during the civil war, and I have forgotten a lot. I have forgotten the names of many fine, courageous men devoted to our cause who fought with me. So I will confine myself to those events, from among what my memory has preserved, that seem to me most typical of the period.

August, 1919: Denikin's troops were advancing on Kiev from the south and Petlyura's men from the west. The cavalry squadron of the Kiev Fortress Regiment in which I served was defending the approaches to Kiev near the small town and railway station of Brovary. At first we fought on foot in the lines; then we were ordered to deliver a cavalry attack. Our squadron was small but we did attack, and so successfully that we captured the enemy positions and took several prisoners. My horse was hit twice and together we toppled into a ditch, almost crushing a White who was taking cover there. He surrendered immediately. Having lost my horse I took off the saddle, put it on my prisoner's shoulders and ordered him to march in the direction I indicated. To lose a horse and, even worse, a saddle, was at that time considered a great misfortune for a cavalryman: there being no horses or saddles in reserve, he would usually be sent off to join the infantry. In this battle, however, we lost more men than horses. By evening I had a new horse, and an even better one.

The next day I was sent to make contact with a neighbouring unit. I already had considerable military experience, so that I was not at all surprised at my commander's words when he said, 'They should be over there—in the wood or somewhere near it.'

I had no trouble crossing the field but I approached the wood with great caution. As I entered it I suddenly heard singing. I stopped and tried to spot the singer. It was a man in civilian clothes with a rifle slung across his back and a broad red ribbon on his chest. I asked him where our nearest infantry were, and he replied, 'Follow the edge of the wood. You'll see them there.'

I rode another five hundred yards or so and saw thirty infantrymen. They were shouting and swearing. They had their rifles slung on their backs and they seemed to be on the point of setting off somewhere. They were arguing fiercely about something among themselves. As I drew near I could hear what they said. 'What good are you to us? On your way with you! We can do without you,' and so on.

At thirty yards I asked, 'Are you from such-and-such regiment?' The answer was 'Yes', in unison, then, 'What are you after?' I ignored the question and asked for their commander. It was the man whom the others had been insulting and threatening who answered. He made a move towards me but they roughly held him back.

The snatches of talk which I had overheard had made me suspicious. I was ready for anything that might happen—wisely, as it turned out. One of those who had been shouting loudest grabbed my horse's bridle and told me to dismount. I drew my sword. 'Keep away from my horse,' I said firmly, and lunged at him. He drew back and I galloped off out of the wood. I heard several shots behind me.

Next morning we heard that an infantry platoon on our left, in the wood, had gone over to the Whites after killing their commander. I then realised what would have happened to me if I had dismounted. In those days the Red Army was occasionally infiltrated by anarchists, semi-delinquents or just plain bandits, and they did much evil.

When we drew back towards Chernigov under pressure from Denikin's army our squadron included many young workers who had volunteered although they had had no previous army service. They were ready to die for the cause, but they had no idea how to shoot properly, how to use a sabre, or even how to ride, and had only the vaguest notion of cavalry drill and military discipline. The squadron commander and the political instructor were both thoroughly devoted men who took advantage of any lull in the fighting to teach the men what they most needed to know.

One day the squadron commander was drilling us. I found myself beside him during a break, out of earshot of the ranks, and suggested that the cavalry manual might be better for teaching than his method was. He listened to me attentively for a while, then said, 'I didn't serve in the cavalry and I don't know cavalry drill. You teach them. Let's see how you get on.'

I took over the drill lesson. The commander watched me carefully and, when I had finished, said, 'You taught them well. You look after the cavalry side in future and I'll teach rifle work.' In the evening he called for me and asked discreetly, 'You're not one of them are you? One of those that used to be . . . ?' I told him I was not and he calmed down.

Under pressure from the Whites, who greatly outnumbered us, our squadron was compelled to leave the village of Yaduty and fall back on the next village. Our commander was told off by headquarters for this and ordered to retake Yaduty. By this time I had won his confidence to some extent and he consulted me about what we were to do.

First, a reconnaissance was necessary; three of us volunteered. Our plan was simple. We skirted the village to the left, under cover of some brushwood, and emerged in the rear of the enemy. I went up and asked the first peasant we saw working in the fields how many Whites had gone into the village. 'Plenty. Heaps,' he answered in broad Ukrainian. 'A hundred?' I suggested. 'Three hundred? Five hundred?' Whatever number I suggested his answer was the same: 'More, many more.'

I returned to my comrades and told them the news. They decided this was evidence enough; it would be absurd to attack the village with only one squadron. But I had an idea—why not make a dash through the village from this side (the enemy's rear), and find out the enemy's strength for ourselves? I reckoned the enemy would not have time to fire a single shot at us. Although my plan was admittedly a little on the reckless side my comrades fell in with it.

We approached the village at a walk, then spurred our horses and galloped down the street brandishing our swords and yelling 'Hurrah!' There were in fact large numbers of Whites in the village, some sitting outside the huts, others standing about in groups or walking up and down the wide street. When they saw us they scattered in all directions like the splash from a puddle you stamp in and went to ground in the gardens at the back. We had counted on being taken for the leading men of an attack from the rear and reckoned that they would not dare try to stop us.

When we had been in possession of this village our squadron commander had been billeted in the priest's house. As it was the best house in the village we were sure that the officers and headquarters would be there. Success had gone to our heads and we decided to make the most of the occasion. We galloped up to the priest's house and

Nikolai and I jumped down from our horses, threw the reins to
Seriozha and dashed into the house to see the backsides of the
officers diving into the garden. We each grabbed an attaché
case and I also seized a revolver which was lying on the table.

Then we were off again, yelling and charging through the
village, with the reins and the cases we had taken in our
left hands and our naked swords in our right. We knew we
would run into the greatest danger as we left the village and
made for our lines; the Whites facing their front would be
ready to open fire instantly. They were so aghast, however,
when we burst out from behind them that we galloped across
the bridge over the stream that marked the village boundary
without hearing a single shot. Only when we were three
hundred yards from the village did we hear the first rifle
shots, and then machine-gun fire. We were back without a
scratch, and with trophies to boot. The cases contained clean
linen, just what we needed as we had none spare and were
much plagued by vermin. I kept the revolver, although it
was an old-fashioned one, until 1937. It reminded me of my
youth and our cheeky exploit. Shortly after this I was given
command of a troop.

Our squadron was merged with the cavalry regiment of
the 60th Rifle Division. On one occasion the regiment was
attacking a village without success. The commanders were
gathered by the roadside around Akulov, the regimental
commander, to discuss the situation. Darkness was falling;
our quarters for the night must be taken into account. It was
too far to go all the way back, and too cold to spend the
night in the fields. The commanders thought that another
attempt should be made to capture the village. I suggested
that if there was to be a frontal assault, one squadron should
strike from a flank. The regimental commander, sucking on
his pipe, strolled up to me and said, 'And who might *you* be?'

'Troop Commander of No. 3 Squadron,' I answered.

'And your idea is—one squadron from the flank?'

'Yes,' I said.

We were then told to attack the village again in an hour and a half, and turning to me the regimental commander added, 'As for you, try to make your way across country and strike their rear flank. Just make as much noise as you can.'

In this village one street ran in from the north to the church and two other streets branched out from the church to the south and the south-east. The enemy's line of retreat lay to the south. When the regiment began its attack our troop forced its way into that part of the village which spread towards the south-east. Shouting and firing we took the first ten houses and drove the Whites, who were only putting up a weak resistance, towards the church. Within the hour the enemy had been cleared out of the village. We spent the night there. Our troop's contribution to the capture of the village is difficult to assess, but from that night the regimental commander began to take some notice of me and soon I was given command of a squadron.

At the end of 1919 I became a member of the Party. At that time I knew nothing about Marxism. All I knew was that Lenin was bitterly hated by all the rich and their hangers-on because he had devoted the whole of his life to the struggle against capitalism, and to the creation of a brighter future for the workers and the poor. For a long time I had been convinced that one must follow only Lenin, stay with the Communists. It was precisely this high idea of the Communist calling which had forced me to postpone my entry into the Party. This is what I thought: Communists must, like Lenin, live for others, and I have not reached this stage; I want to live for myself; I want to live better than I do at present. Later I came to understand that if I was ever to improve, being a member of the Party led by Lenin and working together with my Communist comrades would help me to do so. And if I must die, then better to die a Communist.

On March 1st, 1920, the 17th Cavalry Division, formed from different cavalry regiments, was moved to the area of Novograd–Volynski. Our regiment, now the 100th Cavalry Regiment, held the area around the villages of Katyukha, Klara and Andreevichi, the latter, with its railway station, being defended by our squadron. Later, under enemy pressure, we fell back to the village of Katyukha.

I felt that the 17th Cavalry Division must retrieve the situation, and so was delighted when our regimental commander asked me to find a guide who knew this wood and the homesteads well. I had my eye on a man who had earlier offered himself for this purpose, but he lived at Andreevichi, which was occupied by Polish troops. I said that I could bring him in. The regimental commander pointed out the difficulties of the undertaking, but nevertheless agreed.

The next night, with one trooper, I set out. The night was clear and there was a little frost. We made our way avoiding the paths through the forest, making use of cuttings and marching by the compass. It took us two and a half hours to cover four miles. When we came out to the edge of the forest the village lay before us on a hillock. Not far from the road stood a mill. Further on we passed through a hollow. When we were some two hundred yards to the right of the mill we noticed two Polish sentries standing by it.

There was not a sound in the village. We had to find the church because the man we were looking for lived beside it. In the windows of one house, a little more prosperous-looking than the rest, dim lights were burning. I glanced through a window and saw soldiers asleep on the floor.

Unnoticed we walked up to the house we wanted and quietly tapped on the window. Only after the third tap did we hear something rustle. At last a man's voice asked from inside, 'What do you want?' Calling him by his first name I gave my own name. Silence again, then subdued voices. At last the door opened. I went in, leaving the trooper under cover by the door.

When I explained my object in coming the man's wife burst into tears. 'How can you do it! I'll not let him go!' Her husband tried to talk her round, then fell silent. Finally he said, 'All right! Let's go. Stop crying, woman, I'll be back soon.'

We said good-bye. I told the woman that we would give them a fine cart-horse for helping us. But she only clung to her husband's neck and wept bitterly, repeating, 'I'll not let him go. I'm not letting him.'

I was beginning to fear that the man would change his mind but he merely said, 'If anyone asks tell them I have gone to buy a horse. And shut the door after us.' We left.

Two days later the division set off in two columns. Our column consisted of two regiments. Using the information provided by the guide our column successfully made its way along the forest paths to the rear of the enemy and destroyed the small enemy garrison in one village. The shooting, however, alerted the enemy in neighbouring villages and we soon came under fire. Enemy troops appeared on our right. Behind us, across a marshy valley, stretched a roadway of logs on which our transport, carts on runners and wheels, had been halted.

The action spread. The enemy had been reinforced and began to push us back towards the log road. The situation was becoming critical. I suggested to the regimental commander that he should send a couple of squadrons into the enemy's rear to divert his attention, and clear the transport convoy from the log road in the meantime, so as to open a line of withdrawal. The regimental and divisional commanders approved of the plan and let me have another squadron.

Taking advantage of clearings in the forest we skirted the enemy's flank and emerged at the rear of his advancing forces. He reacted dramatically to our sudden appearance in his rear, cut short the advance and turned the main forces to the west against us. Our position was now exceptionally difficult. We found ourselves galloping in a long straggling column down a small road with paling fences on either side. On our right we were under fire at a range of thirty or forty yards. I turned to look at the troopers behind me and saw only a few. 'Where are the rest?' I thought, and at that moment received a heavy blow on the side of the head. Blood flowed from my ear and down my cheek. I did not even notice that my sabre had fallen from my hand. All that I realised was that I was wounded in the head and that I might soon lose consciousness.

I pressed the dirty skirt of my greatcoat to my ear and cheek and rode on. I felt that I had only a few minutes more to live and I thought of those who were with me; there's no way back for them now, they're done for without me. . . . I spoke out loud to the man riding nearest to me: 'Do you see those tall trees ahead? Gallop up to them, turn sharp left and keep going east. You'll get home that way.' I felt easier after that. Two troopers rode up to me quickly, ready to catch me if I began to fall. But we were already at the trees and I was still in the saddle. They were no longer firing at us.

I was helped from my horse and bandaged up somehow or other and we settled down to wait for those who had fallen behind. Presently we sent a patrol on ahead, set off east-wards and three hours later rejoined our unit. On the way back I kept worrying about the heavy losses in the two squadrons which set out with me and cursed myself that I had not let our guide go in time. The guide was the first person I asked about when I met the regimental commander. He told me that the guide had already been sent home with the horse he had been promised. Then I reported our engagement and the losses we had suffered and was delighted to learn that the squadron which had been temporarily attached to me and the part of my squadron I had given up for lost had come under heavy fire but had rejoined the regiment more than an hour ago. The regimental commander told us that the blow we had delivered had been extremely successful. The Poles had halted their advance and the regiment had been able to withdraw without trouble. Despite my fears the casualties in the two squadrons had been few—one killed and five wounded, including myself. My wound was clean from side to side; the bullet had entered my cheek under the right eye and gone out behind the ear without touching the bone. But for the loss of blood I felt fine.

As I lay in my hospital bed I often recalled that moment when I had been hit. Once again war was forcing me to think! Why, when I was expecting death, did I not regret saying good-bye to life? Why hadn't my thoughts turned to my parents, my home, the people closest to me? Apparently the thought of those who were fighting alongside me and might at any moment have fallen to a enemy bullet dominated me too strongly to spare a thought for myself. At that moment I was indeed thinking of those closest to me, because in battle nobody is closer than one's comrades-in-arms. Could it be that I had already succeeded in learning at least something through being a member of Lenin's Party? I examined my conscience—what was it that was new in me? —and although I could find no definite answer the very

thought that I, Sanka Gorbatov, was a Communist, a
member of Lenin's Party, gave me satisfaction.

I spent two weeks in hospital at Zhitomir, and on April 1st
returned to my regiment, then stationed in the village of
Kanneny Brod, south-east of Novograd–Volyansk.

After withdrawing over the Dnieper the 17th Cavalry
Division was broken up and its elements re-formed as two
cavalry regiments, one joining the 7th and the other the
58th Rifle Division. I was appointed deputy commander of
the Cavalry Regiment, 58th Rifle Division, but in fact
commanded the regiment myself since the C.O., Comrade
Akulov, was ill for a long time. We were defending the
eastern bank of the Dnieper south of Darnitsa, almost as far
as Tripolye.

That June I very nearly lost my life again. The regiment
I was commanding was ordered by Kniagnitski, commander of the 58th Rifle Division, to force a crossing of the
Dnieper, which was at that time almost overflowing with
the spring flood. After a preliminary reconnaissance we
reported to the divisional commander that the task was
impossible: even if the regiment managed to cross it would
be in no condition to fight afterwards. 'Cross that river or the
regimental commander gets shot!' was his reply. My horse
was the strongest so I agreed to make the test, and in doing
so experienced the awful, utter loneliness of an imminent
and futile death, quite different from the feeling you get
when you are charging into battle with your men at your
back. My horse slipped from under me and struggled back
to the bank. I only just reached a sandbank in the middle
of the river before the water closed over my head. I rested
on the sandbank for a while and then plunged back into
the fearful current and returned to the eastern bank. I

reported the whole adventure to the divisional commander and after that even he no longer insisted on forcing the river.

Until August, 1919, the Independent Bashkir Brigade, the 27th and 28th Cavalry Regiments, had been part of Kolchak's army stationed in the village of Turkmen in the region of Verkhne–Uralsk. On August 19th the officers and men supporting the revolution arrested the counter-revolutionary officers and crossed to the Red Army under the command of Comrade Murtazin. In a very short time the Bashkirs made a name for themselves as staunch fighters in the Soviet cause. The 1st Bashkir Cavalry Regiment, also formed from men who had served in Kolchak's army, joined the Red Army in the beginning of 1919 after killing those officers who were not prepared to serve the people. Later it was thrown into the fighting around Petrograd where it acquitted itself well.

The Independent Bashkir Brigade was sent from the Eastern Front to the area east of Kiev in April, 1920. In May, the 1st Bashkir Cavalry Regiment joined it from Petrograd. On June 1st the Brigade forced the Dnieper and together with the 7th Rifle Division under its exceptionally daring and talented commander, Golikov, drove forward until on August 15th they took the town of Ustilug on the Western Bug. Just after the fall of Koviel I was appointed to command the 2nd Bashkir Cavalry Brigade.

The brigade surged on ahead of the rifle regiments, forced the Western Bug and captured Grubeshov. The Poles had left this town in a great hurry and abandoned great stores of vodka and spirits in the distillery. My first inkling of this came from the huge number of drunks littering the gutters or wandering aimlessly around the streets. At the distillery a terrible scene of wholesale and complete drunkenness met me. A deafening din of shouts and curses hung over it. Dead to the world, men were clinging to the huge vats, struggling, pushing, knocking each other away to get at the liquor. We had the greatest trouble getting the warehouse and the distillery yard cleared of people, the doors locked and a sentry posted on guard. Within the hour the sentry was drunk and the townsfolk, not only the Red Army soldiers, were making off with the liquor. We opened the vats and let the spirits run out over the ground. Within a few hours the whole garrison was drunk. Even the officers wandered about in a daze. I seemed to be the only person sober. I climbed the town's watchtower to look for any signs of approaching enemy and waited fretfully for my subordinates' heads to clear. The hours never seemed so long as they did then. This was a very unusual incident in the brigade, and there was never another like it. On the contrary, Bashkir discipline was always very high, both in and out of battle. But the green dragon of liquor is a strong dragon indeed.

For a short time the front was static. Our forces held a bridgehead over the Western Bug. Two of our regiments were in forward positions, the third was in reserve. Infantry held the line to our right. Then we received the order to advance at dawn and occupy all centres of population within fifteen miles.

Thirty minutes after the last squadrons of our two regiments had disappeared from view Commissar Kuzminski and I set out with a troop of eighteen men. We made our way up the Western Bug to join the third regiment and with them follow the other two. Suddenly thirty horsemen appeared on our left, trotting towards us in open order. On seeing us they slowed to a walk. We were surprised to see men riding east in military formation and on closer inspection saw that they were Poles. 'Enemy scouts,' we thought, 'probing in depth.' This would never do, so we decided to attack although we were outnumbered. I gave the order: 'Troop, in line abreast. Draw sabres. Follow me. Charge!'

The Poles halted. Only two hundred yards separated us when a large column of riders emerged from a ravine behind our enemies. 'Left wheel!' I shouted, and back we galloped to the village which we had just left. I decided to gallop to the centre of the village and then north to where our third regiment was stationed. With its help we could destroy the enemy. The road led through a narrow gulley with steep sides. Seventy Poles were close behind us. Then, to our joy, some forty riders appeared in front of us. 'The regiment knows,' I thought. 'That's their leading detachment.' But the men riding towards us, obviously reckoning us, and the Poles rattling full tilt after us, as one mass of enemy, took fright. There was no turning back in that narrow gulley so they tried to let us through, clambering up the steep banks at the sides, some of them even falling from their horses. It was only as we dashed through them that I saw that they were not our Bashkirs at all, but Poles who had lost their way!

We found ourselves in a field. Commissar Kuzminski set off eastward with the headquarters platoon, while my orderly and I made for the village where our regiment was stationed. Most of the Poles went after the Commissar, while fifteen or so chased me. Presently our horses began to flag and I was relieved to see our regiment coming out from the village and machine-guns being set up. They opened fire on the Poles—and on me! Only when the Poles turned back and I went on towards the village did the firing stop. Great was the confusion of the regimental commander when he recognised his brigade commander!

Those of our troopers who had the best mounts set about clearing the field. Then an enemy column appeared and our men began to fall back. At a signal from me they rallied round me and I formed them, some two hundred and fifty in all, in a single line facing the enemy. The senior Polish officer had about an equal number and did the same. There were twenty or thirty yards between him and me, fifty between our men. There was complete silence except for the repeated orders to charge, from him and from me, and the jangling of stirrups and sabres as our excited horses moved uneasily. Neither side could make up its mind to attack first. I know quite well that the Polish officer might get his men to move first, and it was equally clear that the first to charge would sweep the field.

Our voices were hoarse as we again gave the order to charge, but the opposing ranks stood still. There is no telling how this might have ended if I had not suddenly acted very peculiarly. I sheathed my sabre without taking my eyes off the Polish officer. I noticed a satisfied smile flit across his face—he obviously thought I was a former Tsarist officer with anti-Soviet leanings and believed that I was about to give myself up. Instead I snatched my pistol from its holster, dug in my spurs, fired at him and yelled, 'Take that! Die, dog!'

I fired at him three times. The Pole hauled his horse round and turned tail. His troopers tried to follow him, and those on the flanks succeeded. Those in the middle, however, were too closely packed to follow and we crashed in among them. We took nearly two hundred prisoners, including two officers, with only three shots!

In the wars of 1918–1920 cavalry actions such as these were not infrequent. Today they sound like stories from olden times.

My memory selects from those years incidents that in some measure had a bearing on my later life. Two such episodes, two mistakes I made, have haunted me through the years. In both cases I came to regard myself as the victim of the mistakes of others.

The senior intelligence officer of the brigade was a man called Vinogradov. I took a dislike to him at first sight. He was a ginger-haired man with one leg shorter than the other. He had studied at the Gatchina Military Academy in Tsarist days. He was well-educated, intelligent and a good soldier, but in spite of all this I distrusted him.

Once, during a retreat, I was leaving a village at dawn with five troopers. Between us and the enemy there was only a mounted patrol. On the road out of the village a man was limping along with a case in his hand. I recognised Vinogradov. 'He wants to be taken prisoner by the Poles!' I thought. 'He didn't know that I was still about.' I was so angry I even had no desire to swear or spit at him. 'Let him stay,' I thought. 'That's one skunk less!' I rode past him without a word, just staring into his embarrassed face.

The next night I saw him again. It turned out that he had slept in his billet, only to discover when he awoke that we had all left. He had hurried after us. I felt ashamed that I had ridden past him without a word, and had not even taken his case, lame as he was. Worst of all, I had suspected him of the meanest intentions. This troubled my conscience for a long time.

I have also come to realise that a first, deceptive impression can lodge in one for a long time even after one has realised one's mistake. Working with Vinogradov for several years I came to know how conscientious and hard-working he was. Then he went on leave to the Bashkir Republic and was arrested on the night of his return and accused of espionage. He spent five months in the death cell. The Special Department informed me that every time Vinogradov had gone on leave he had been to Poland. It was clear that he had been working for Pilsudsky. All my old suspicions returned—my first impression had been the right one. But when, a month after his release, Comrade Vinogradov returned to the regiment, he told me that he had been arrested by mistake, and related the following story.

Returning from leave he had travelled in the train with a man with whom he had played chess. His new acquaintance turned out to be a member of the *Cheka*. The secret police in Zhitomir had for a long time been looking for a man with the same set of names. After five months in prison Vinogradov was finally brought before the interrogator. Walking into the room he saw, seated beside the interrogator, a man who stared at him intently and said, 'No, that's not him. That's not the one I know.' Three days later he was released.

And now the other incident, apparently quite unrelated to the first but equally significant to me and akin to it in my experience. I thought about these two things a lot, later.

In 1920, during a long halt in a forest, I was informed that a young Pole had been captured. When he was asked to explain why he was in the forest the young man said that he was looking for a cow which he had lost and that he was a peasant from a village a couple of miles away. He claimed to have lived in this village all his life, but when I asked him the names of villages in the vicinity he could not give a single one. To frighten him, I turned to a trooper with the order: 'Shoot him.' At that moment I was called away on business.

Some minutes later I remembered the prisoner. I knew the Bashkirs and their unquestioning discipline and, afraid that they might indeed shoot him, I ordered him to be brought back. Too late: the shots rang out as I spoke and I was told that the spy was dead. I was ninety-nine per cent. certain that he was a spy, but although in all my wars I have with my own hands killed, shot, sabred and hacked, that one

per cent. of doubt made me deeply regret my rash order.
Eighteen years later I had cause to regret it still more.

For my part in the battles with the Poles I was awarded
the Order of the Red Banner. Then, the Polish war over, the
brigade was transferred to the south to deal with the Petlyuna
gangs. Later I was given the task of liquidating three groups
of bandits in the regions of Tulchinsk, Bratslava and Gaysin.

Large-scale demobilisation took place during the summer
of 1921 in the course of which the 12th Bashkir Cavalry
Regiment was formed and I was appointed its commander.

Looking back I realise that the names of many brave men
from those days have escaped my memory. But let me call
to mind Faizulin Khusmetdin Sharanovich, the daring and
resourceful commander of the 27th Cavalry Regiment;
Ashranov, an unhurried, thoughtful, fearless soldier; Mar-
tazin Ibragim, who had met a soldier's death before I joined
the brigade, but was as alive for me as if we had actually met,
through the tales told by his Bashkir comrades; Garapov
Usnan, a resolute, honest military commander; the political
workers, Brigade Commissar Kuzminski, Regimental Com-
missars Kuchaev and Komalov Gali. The whole brigade
knew the courage and Communist devotion of Squadron
Commanders Ishmuratov, Zayanchurin, Kazanbaev and
Gafurov. And there are many, many more whose names I
have forgotten. So many of them survived enemy bullets only
to find death in the years after 1937.

When the war was over and the bandits had been dealt
with I did not think that I would remain in the Red Army.
I imagined that, in peacetime, commanders better educated
and better versed in military affairs than I would take my
place. But the fates and the Party willed that I should remain
in the army, and I have served in it to this day.

SIX

Peacetime Soldier

On March 1st, 1921, the Revolutionary Military Council of
the Republic, in its Order No. 504, declared:

1. The assessment of the fitness of commanding personnel
   to hold their appointments and to be put forward for
   promotion . . . shall be based upon their military
   record and their loyalty to the Soviet Power. If, in
   his present post, the leader under consideration has
   shown himself capable of directing his unit in the
   military situation of the Revolutionary War, and
   demonstrated that he is a loyal worker in the Soviet
   cause, this clearly indicates his fitness for the appointment he occupies, as well as the possibility of promotion to a higher appointment. . . .
2. Particular attention should be paid to the assessment
   of those leaders who were promoted to positions of
   command from the ranks of the Red Army during the
   Revolutionary War. They are particularly valuable to
   the army. If in theoretical knowledge of military
   matters such persons are deficient, it is essential to
   raise their standard of military education. . . .
3. Commanding personnel who are experienced in
   training matters but have no operational experience
   should not be allowed precedence over those who have

displayed special capabilities in commanding troops under operational conditions. . . .

In accordance with this order, signed by E. Skliansky and S. Kamenev, I remained in the army and was appointed regimental commander.

In 1912, when my army service began, a regiment would be housed in barracks with stables. Contractors provided hay and firewood for the regiment; victuals and uniforms were regularly delivered to the regimental stores. There were riding halls, messes, firing ranges, and the officers had their own quarters. Training was according to well-established plans and instructions.

In 1922 the regiment was billeted in the villages and everything was correspondingly different. This demanded incomparably more work from the commanding officer. I was worried because I had spent only three winters at school, while the commanding officers of the neighbouring regiments had a secondary education, or at any rate the beginnings of it. True, I was conscious of a certain advantage over them: I was already thirty years old, and ten of those years had been spent in the army. The answer was to teach my subordinates what I knew and learn myself what I needed to acquire.

In the winter of 1925 I was called to Moscow to a meeting of senior cavalry leaders. From my 'soft' class compartment I saw a tall thick-set man in a greatcoat pass along the corridor. There was something very familiar about him from a long way back. The feeling was so strong that a cold shudder ran down my spine. I got up quickly and went out to look at his face. Yes, I was not mistaken—it was the former Staff Captain Sviderskii, who had so mercilessly instructed us young soldiers in 1912 and 1913.

When I reminded him who I was he said: 'I am very pleased to renew the acquaintance.' And, pointing to my badges of rank, which were the same as his own, he added: 'I'm glad to see that what I taught you was not wasted.'

'The teaching wasn't wasted,' I answered. 'That at least I can thank you for.'

He was chairman of a commission which bought horses for the army in the Soviet Union and abroad and was going to the same meeting as I. He told me that the commissar in his commission was Silindrik, a member of the Party since 1905. I knew Silindrik; he had once served in our division as commissar of one of the regiments.

Sviderskii kept coming into my compartment. He seemed to feel uneasy and was probably trying to remember whether I was one of those whom he had beaten unmercifully and whether I would talk about it in Moscow. When I met Silindrik I told him that I had known Sviderskii from 1912 to 1915 but kept quiet about his treatment of the men. Silindrik had a high opinion of Sviderskii. According to him Sviderskii had been offered the post of director of a state stud farm, with a large salary, during one of his purchasing trips to Germany. He had replied: 'When there was a revolution in Russia some of our officers fled to you. When you have a revolution, where will you run to? No, one revolution is enough for me.'

On the third day of the meeting Sviderskii invited me to dinner. I was interested to see the style in which he lived, as in the old days there were rumours among the men that he was very rich. As it turned out he lived with his wife in two rooms packed tight with furniture and chests stacked up to the ceiling. 'It looks as though he's been "condensed," ' I thought.

Everything went well until I refused to drink wine when

my host proposed a toast to the Red Army and to me as one of its representatives. He refused to believe that a soldier would not drink wine and took my refusal as a personal insult. I had to persuade him that not only did I not drink wine, but I did not even touch beer. In the course of this conversation I had to confess that at first I had been somewhat on my guard against him remembering his excessively severe attitude towards the men. 'Believe me,' I added, 'I was delighted to hear of your honest work for the Soviet Power. No one has the right to drag from the past what you would prefer to forget.'

We shook hands and relaxed. I told him that since the men had believed him to be very rich I was surprised that he was not abroad. His answer was frank: 'My father was a patriot and kept his money in Russian banks; and you know what happened to such money. As for going abroad, the decisive thing was that we lived in Moscow. If we had been in the south we might have been as silly as other people, and shared the bitter plight of the *émigrés*.'

At that time all soldiers studied, some in military academies and colleges, some at courses, some during what should have been their leisure time because their senior officers would not release them. 'What do you want to go studying for? I wouldn't even accept two graduates in your place.' So I was among those who could not get released for study.

I remember those far-off days with pleasure, the friendly teamwork of the regimental staff from the youngest commander to the most senior, the enthusiasm, the urge to win high marks in training. How few minor faults there were, let alone crimes! The guardroom was mostly empty—the military tribunal had no cases to try. At that time no attempt was made to punish simply in order to strengthen discipline. The whole emphasis was on the creation of conditions which would make for the prevention of crime, a task everybody was engaged in, not only the commanders and the political workers but members of military tribunals, detectives, doctors, every Party member and every Young Communist. I remember how much I would take to heart the slightest hint of some defect in the work of the regiment when it was made by a senior commander. I would lose my appetite and my sleep, worrying about my failure to notice the fault myself.

We often took part in tactical games organised by the military district and I was always surprised by the youthfulness of District Commander I. E. Yakir, and by his ability, during the discussions at the end, to put what he had to say in such a way that nobody could develop a swollen head, yet none of the senior commanders present could feel that their authority had been undermined. When discussing a correct solution he would not only point out how it fitted the conditions of the problem, but would draw attention to other possibilities that had not been taken into account. If the solution he was analysing did not meet the needs of the situation he always tried to find in it at least a trace of merit. Above all he always guarded the faith of his subordinates in their own judgment. I would return from these exercises feeling enriched and more knowledgeable.

In 1928 I became a brigade commander in the 3rd Cavalry Division, an appointment that pleased me because I had commanded a regiment for seven years, and that seemed long enough.

In 1933 I was appointed to command the 4th Turkestan Mountain Cavalry Division and joined the army commander in Tashkent. My new division did well, and I seemed in those days to be in such good spirits that nothing in the world could darken them.

In May, 1936, I suddenly received the order to take over the 2nd Cavalry Division in which for seven years, until the autumn of 1928, I had commanded a regiment. When I went to see Yakir in Kiev, he said to me: 'Fascism in Germany is growing more shameless every day. We must be ready for anything.' This was exactly what 1 felt, so that it was an additional cause for pleasure to find that the 2nd Division was better equipped than the Turkmen Division I had left. Besides an armoured squadron it already included a tank regiment with new fast tanks. The quality of the artillery had been improved, one of the cavalry regiments and been motorised, and so on.

Our cavalry division was under the patronage of the German Communist Party. Wilhelm Pieck, a member of the Executive Committee of the Comintern, who had lived a long time in Moscow, visited us every year at the May 1st and November 7th holidays. One evening in November, 1936, at supper at my quarters, he offered a toast to our future meeting in 'Berlin freed from Fascism.' My wife drank the toast for me. That dream seemed hopelessly far off then.

Manoeuvres took place in the area of Shepetovka in 1936, at the end of the summer. Yakir was in charge, and Voroshilov and Budienny were present. Afterwards a riding competition was held in Kiev. At a meeting in the Kiev Opera House one evening all the marshals of the Soviet Union made their appearance. This meeting between the best of the Ukraine and the highest representatives of the army was a moving and heartfelt occasion. Who could have guessed that we were seeing some of these marshals for the last time?

Part Three

SEVEN

The Black Year

Opening the paper one spring morning in 1937 I read that the organs of State Security 'had uncovered a Fascist military plot.' Among the conspirators named were several leading Soviet military figures, including Marshal of the Soviet Union M. N. Tukhachevsky.

This news simply stunned me. 'How can it be,' I thought, 'that men who took such a part in routing foreign interventionists and internal reactionaries, men who have done so much to improve our army, Communists tested in the leanest days—how can it be that they have suddenly become enemies of the people?' Finally, after mulling over a host of possible explanations, I accepted the answer most common in those days. 'No matter how you feed the wolf, it will always look towards the forest,' as the saying goes. There was some apparent justification for this, since Tukhachevsky and a number of those arrested with him came from rich families and had been Tsarist officers. 'Obviously,' many people said at the time, trying to puzzle out an answer, 'they fell into the nets of foreign intelligence organisations while abroad on duty or to take a cure.'

At the Kiev District Party Conference many of us noticed that I. E. Yakir, usually so gay and full of life, looked morose and tense at the Praesidium table. Many accounted for this by the rumours of his transfer to commander of the Leningrad military district, a less important post. Some days later we heard that Yakir had been arrested in a train somewhere not far from Moscow as a member of the 'Tukhachevsky Conspiratorial Group.' This was a terrible blow. I knew Yakir well and respected him. Deep down, I nursed a hope that it was only a mistake—'It will be sorted out and he will go free'—but this was the sort of thing that only the closest friends risked saying among themselves.

Soon the Kiev military district was put under new command. Shchadenko, the Military Council member, showed his suspicions of the headquarters staff from the very first. He scrutinised the commanders and political workers of the units and without even bothering to conceal it, and without much delay, working hand in glove with the Special Department, set in motion a vigorous campaign to compromise the commanders. This resulted in the mass arrest of senior commanders and political workers. With each arrest it became more difficult to believe in the disloyalty, the sabotage, the treachery of these men, yet what was one to believe or disbelieve? Not a day passed without fresh reports in the papers of even more startling facts about new incidents of sabotage, subversion and spying. When, early in August, 1937, the commander of our 7th Cavalry Corps, Petr Petrovich Grigorev, was urgently called to Kiev, the commanders in the division began to worry. I heard that he was due home that evening and telephoned his wife to tell her that I would come to see him on the following day.

When my wife and I arrived at the Grigorevs we found them in deep gloom. The reason for his call to Kiev, so Petr Petrovich told me, was that he had been accused in the District Party Committee of contacts with enemies of the people. When we were about to leave Maria Andreevna burst into tears and Grigorev said as we shook hands: 'Who knows whether we'll see each other again?'

I wanted to say something to reassure him. 'You have nothing to worry about. You—a working man's son!' I told him. 'Get rid of that long face; this will all be sorted out in Kiev.' But when we left the Grigorevs we were sad, and we stayed silent all the way to Staro-Konstantinov with only one, obvious thought uppermost in our minds. Next day we learned that Grigorev had been arrested. The same day my division was visited by the head of the Corps political department, Bogdanov. He summoned the division to a meeting and declared that the corps commander had been proved to be an 'enemy of the people.'

'Had proved to be . . .' In those days this was a sort of magic spell which was supposed to account for everything; a man had lived, had worked and then, suddenly, 'had proved to be . . .'

I too was called upon to speak. I said that I had known Comrade Grigorev for over fourteen years. During this time we had fought anti-Party deviations together. Grigorev had never once vacillated on points of Party policy. He was one of the best commanders in the whole army. If he had ever become alienated from the Party it would have shown, especially to me, one of his closest subordinates for so many years. I was certain that Grigorev's case would be cleared up after investigation and that his innocence would be proved. Those who spoke after me stressed Grigorev's excessive 'fault-finding,' as they called it—which meant in plain terms that he was an efficient and challenging commander—and they tried to pick on defects in his work.

After the meeting Bogdanov, the head of the corps political department, and Kulikov, the head of the divisional political department, accused me of 'liberalism.' Of all those who attended the meeting only my wife said that I had spoken justly and truly.

A day or so later I was informed that the commander of the 7th Cavalry Regiment had given away his splendidly trained horse, a horse that had won first prizes at military district competitions, to the representative of the Special Department, who could not even ride properly. I would never have dreamed that this commander could have sunk so low. I summoned him to my headquarters and told him: 'You obviously have something on your conscience; that's why you're currying favour with the Special Department. Get that horse back immediately or it will be wrecked by a rider who doesn't know how to treat it.' The next day the divisional commander telephoned me to say that my order had been carried out.

Another month passed. Then, by order of the military district commander, I was removed from the command of the division and shortly afterwards expelled from the Party by the district headquarters organisation, for contacts with 'enemies of the people'. I was placed at the disposal of the Chief Directorate of Personnel of the People's Commissariat of Defence.

My wife and I talked it over and decided to leave for Moscow. At first we took a room at the Central Red Army Hotel; then, having stored our things and obtained permission from the Chief Directorate, we set off for Saratov to stay with my wife's parents, as we did not have enough money to live in the hotel. My father-in-law, Aleksandr Vasilevich Veselov, and his wife, Lyubov Sergeevna, who was the soul of kindness, welcomed us most warmly. Aleksandr Vasilevich was at that time head of the Movements Branch in the Ryazan–Ural Railway. With them lived their daughter, Lina, a student at a medical institute, and their son, Seriozha, a pupil at a secondary school. They occupied a three-roomed flat and very kindly lent us one room.

For another few months my situation remained uncertain. Then, early in March, 1938, I was summoned to the Chief Political Directorate and reinstated in the Party. As a result of this my treatment at the Chief Directorate of Personnel changed radically. Two and a half months later, on May 15th, I was appointed deputy commander of the 6th Cavalry Corps, under G. K. Zhukov. We were beside ourselves with joy. True enough, I would have much preferred my own command, because by nature I like independent work, but I had not been given one. 'It looks as if I am still under a shadow,' I thought. 'Ah well, no matter . . .'

We set off for the town of Osipovichi, at that time the headquarters of the 6th Cavalry Corps. The corps commander made us welcome and lodged us on the second floor of the detached house in which he lived. I had missed my work and I quickly set to. Soon afterwards Zhukov was appointed deputy commander for cavalry of the military district and went to Smolensk, leaving me as acting corps commander for a time. I assumed that I would be confirmed in this post, but my hopes were not realised. 'So my suspicions are confirmed,' I thought. 'I am still under a shadow.'

In September the corps storekeeper sent me a message that I should collect my winter uniform. I went to see him the following day. He looked thoroughly embarrassed as he showed me a telegram from the corps commissar, Senior Political Instructor Fominykh, who was at that time in Moscow. 'REFRAIN FROM ISSUING WINTER UNIFORM TO GORBATOV.' Shortly after this strange telegram an order came putting me on the reserve.

Twenty-three years later, to take a glimpse into the future, in the spring of 1962, a lieutenant-general came up to the group of generals and senior officers in which I was standing and said to me: 'I have a feeling, Comrade Gorbatov, that you don't recognise me. I am Fominykh, former commissar of the 6th Cavalry Corps. I've long since retired and am living in Leningrad.'

'Yes, Comrade Fominykh,' I answered. 'I did not recognise you at first, but I did think that I had seen you somewhere. Now I remember you. I remember you particularly well when you were corps commissar, with the rank of senior political instructor, and you sent a telegram from Moscow suggesting I should not be issued with a winter uniform. It was some days later that I was relieved of my post, and you know what happened then.'

Fominykh was not pleased that he had renewed the acquaintance.

So, on October 15th, 1938, I left Osipovichi for Moscow to try and find out why I had been expelled from the army. I was not allowed to see the People's Commissar, but on October 21st the head of the Chief Directorate of Personnel, Shchadenko, listened to me for a couple of minutes and said: 'We'll try and find out what your position is.' He asked me where I was staying.

That afternoon I sent my wife a telegram: 'POSITION BEING CLARIFIED.' At two in the morning there was a knock at the door of my hotel room.

'Who's there?' I called.

A woman's voice answered: 'A telegram for you.'

'Obviously from my wife,' I thought, as I opened the door.

Three uniformed men came into the room and one of them told me point-blank that I was under arrest. I demanded to see his warrant. 'Can't you see for yourself who we are?' he replied. Thereupon one began to tear the medals off my tunic, and another to cut the badges of rank from my uniform, while the third watched me dress. They took away my Party card, my identity papers and all my other documents. They escorted me out of the hotel. They pushed me into a car. We travelled in silence. I cannot describe what I felt as the car hurtled in the early morning through the empty streets of Moscow.

First the massive gates of the Lubyanka closed behind me and then the door of my cell. I could vaguely see some people in there and I greeted them. Their voices answered me in chorus. There were seven of them. After a short silence, one of them said: 'Our army comrade is probably thinking: "I am not guilty of anything and here I am among state criminals." It's no use thinking that. We are just like you. Don't be shy. Sit down on your bunk and tell us what is happening in the world. We haven't heard anything for a long time.'

What seemed to interest my comrades-in-misfortune most was the situation in Hitler's Germany. Gradually I came to know that at one time they had all held responsible positions. They impressed me as being cultured and serious-minded people. I was all the more horrified to hear that during their interrogations every single one of them had written the most unmitigated rubbish, confessing to imaginary crimes and incriminating other people. Some had given way under physical pressure; some had been terrified merely by threats of torture.

This I simply could not understand. 'It is not only you and those against whom you have falsely testified who will suffer,' I told them. 'It is your relatives and your friends. Besides, you are misleading the investigations and therefore the Soviet authorities.'

But they found my arguments unconvincing. Some even held the strange theory that the more people were jailed the sooner it would be realised that all this was nonsense and harmful to the Party.

'No,' I said, 'under no circumstances will I do what you have done.'

As they tried to justify themselves at first I felt some sympathy, but gradually these cowards became repulsive to me. I was angry: 'Just by your lying alone you have committed a serious crime. That's why you're being kept in prison.'

They answered ironically: 'Let's see what you have to say for yourself in a week's time.'

For three days I was not called. Then, on the evening of the fourth day, I was led away to the interrogator. He checked the facts about me, told me to sit down opposite him, gave me pen and paper and said: 'Describe all the crimes you have committed.'

'There's nothing to write,' I replied.

'They all say that at first, then they think better of it. They remember and write. You've plenty of time. We're in no hurry. Those who have nothing to write are outside—free. Now, you just get on and write.' He left the room.

Some hours passed. When he returned and saw I had written nothing he enquired: 'Have you really not understood what's required of you? We don't like jokes around here—remember that, will you? So let's see you write something. It'll do you no good to try things on with me. There's been no one yet who hasn't written for me. Is that clear?' He left the room again.

About an hour later, when he came back and saw I had still not written anything, he said: 'You've made a very bad start. What a shame. Well, think it over back in your cell.'

Two hefty military security guards flung me back into the cell. As soon as the door slammed to behind me I was showered with questions: 'What did they ask?' 'How did you answer?' 'What did you testify to?' They came to the conclusion that the method of interrogation had not changed. I would have to wait for the next session, when I would either write or be sent to Lefortovo.

This proved to be the case. One day, after all that had happened at the first interrogation had been repeated, the interrogator became very rude. He swore at me and threatened to send me to Lefortovo.

That day I was summoned again for a short session. Someone 'higher up the scale' talked to me this time. He asked me to write out a statement, and when I said firmly, 'I shan't,' he too began swearing and ended with the threat: 'You've only yourself to blame.'

The next day the cell door opened and a man came in and asked: 'Surname beginning with G?' I called my name. It was clear then that I was being taken to Lefortovo Prison. The other prisoners expressed their sympathy, gave me some advice and wished me all the best.

I was pushed into a black van. I heard the engine start and the gates slam. From time to time I caught snatches of conversation and laughter from the street. Then I heard the gates of Lefortovo open and shut.

I was put in a cell originally intended for one prisoner. Two other men were there already. There were three bunks, arranged in the form of a U. My neighbours turned out to be Brigade Commander B. and the head of one of the chief committees of the People's Commissariat of Trade, K. Both had already written utter balderdash incriminating themselves and others. They assured me there was no other way out. The stories they told made my hair stand on end. It was unbelievable that anything like this could be happening in Russia. My new colleagues were firm in their opinion— better write straight away. If you didn't sign today you would sign in a week's time or six months' time or some time; it was all the same.

'I'd rather die,' I said, 'than defame myself or—which is much worse—others.'

'That's how we felt when we got here,' was their reply.

Three days passed. The sessions with the interrogator began. At first they were no different from those in the Lubyanka, but when the interrogator had convinced himself that I would not write he hissed: 'You will. They've all written for us so far, and that's the way it's going to be with you.'

The fourth time I was called before one of the senior men. First he asked quietly whether I had any idea of what I was letting myself in for. Had I thought everything out properly, taken everything into account? Then he said to my interrogator: 'Yes, I agree with you!' and left the room.

On this occasion it was a long time before I returned from the interrogation. When, with difficulty, I made my way back to the cell, my comrades said with one voice: 'There you are! That's only the start of it.' Comrade B. said softly, shaking his head: 'What's the good?'

Five interrogations accompanied by torture followed, with intervals of two or three days. Sometimes I had to be helped back to the cell. Then I was given a rest for about twenty days. The thought of my wife disturbed me most of all, but suddenly I received fifty roubles and that gave me grounds for believing that she was free. My fellow prisoners thought that the respite from interrogation was a good sign for me.

But it was not long before the interrogation began again—

another series of five sessions. During one of them I accident-
ally found out that my fiend of an interrogator's name was
Stolbunski. I don't know where he is now. If he is still alive
I hope he will read these lines and feel my contempt for him,
not only now but when I was in his hands. But I think he
knew this well enough. Apart from him, two brawny tor-
turers took part in the interrogation. Even now my ears ring
with the sound of Stolbunski's evil voice hissing 'You'll sign,
you'll sign!' as I was carried out, weak and covered in blood.
I withstood the torture during the second bout of interrogation, but when the third bout started, how I longed to be
able to die!

Once Comrade C. asked me: 'Doesn't even this convince
you that you have no way out?'

'No, it doesn't,' I answered. 'I shall die if necessary, and
as I die I shall repeat it—No! No!'

At last they left me in peace and for three months I was
not interrogated. At that time I firmly believed I would be
freed. More than once I banged on the door and demanded
to see the director of the prison or the prosecutor. Of course,
such impudence did not go unpunished. But one had to
while away the time somehow.

I changed my mind about many things during those three
months. For the first time I was not sorry that my parents
were dead; at least they had not lived to see me arrested. I
often thought of my wife. She was worse off than me. I was,
after all, in the company of other outcasts, whereas she was
among free people among whom there might be many who
would shun her as the wife of an 'enemy of the people.' This
thought gave me no peace.

I remember—it was the last interrogation but one—that
the interrogator asked me what my relations with my wife
were like. I told him they were good.

'Oh, are they? Then we'll arrest her too. We can make her testify against you as well as herself.'

I cursed myself for my frankness. Gradually, though, I was reassured. The fifty roubles continued to arrive each month, showing that she was still free.

As I discovered later, my wife received the telegram I sent the day I was arrested. Several days passed and there was no more news of me. Her uneasiness grew. Finally she went to see the new corps commander.

'They've probably sent him somewhere,' said Andrei Ivanovich Eremenko.

On November 8th she decided to go to Moscow. Before setting off she called on the corps commander again.

'If they had arrested Aleksandr Vasilevich I would have known about it,' said Andrei Ivanovich in reply to her question. Nevertheless he asked the head of the Special Department to come to see him and, in my wife's presence, expressed his fear that I had been arrested.

'If that had happened we would have known about it and searched his quarters long ago,' answered the head of the Special Department, glancing at my wife.

On November 9th my wife came to Moscow. Acquaintances told her that they had last seen me on October 20th and thought that I had gone home. At the hotel she was told that I had left on the 22nd, but as she was leaving a girl caught up with her in the corridor and as she passed without stopping said quietly: 'He was arrested on the night of the 22nd.'

Out in the square opposite the hotel my wife sat down on a bench. She sat there for a long time, weeping and trying to make up her mind what to do next. She decided to go to the Lubyanka. She was sent to the Enquiry Office of the

N.K.V.D. When her turn came in the queue she asked: 'Where is my husband?'

'And what makes you think that your husband has been arrested?' they countered.

'I have had no news from him for a long time.'

'We haven't got your husband.'

However, they did give her the addresses of all the prisons, apart from Lefortovo, and added: 'Look for him yourself. We know nothing about him.'

She got the same answer at the other prisons and at the deportation points. Finally, when she had gone full circle, she returned to the Enquiry Office and once again waited in the queue. It was there that she met a woman who advised her to go to Lefortovo Prison, and gave her some tips about how to find out what she wanted to know. Acting on this advice my wife entered the prison yard, went up to a window and asked the man on duty to take a parcel for Gorbatov. The window slammed shut. Some time later the same man appeared, asked my wife for her passport and took fifty roubles. This was how she learned that I was in Lefortovo Prison. Then she called on our closest friends in Moscow, told them everything she knew and left for home.

On the way my wife decided to leave Osipovichi and go to Saratov, to her mother's place, so that they could share their grief. On April 30th, 1938, my wife's father had been arrested, and a little earlier, in 1937, her brother, who was an engineer. She thought it would be easier to find work in Saratov. As soon as she arrived she told the corps commander of her intention. He approved, and helped her, a rare thing in those days. He also expressed his conviction that I was innocent. It is with deep gratitude that we both remember Eremenko's noble action and his civic courage, hardly less difficult than courage in the field.

On the night before my wife left, at about two in the morning, there was loud knocking at the door of the flat. The servant said tearfully: 'It's for you, Nina Aleksandrovna.' She did not want to open the door herself.

Steeling herself, my wife ran quickly down the stairs and said: 'Who's there?'

'Where's the hotel?' came the response from two drunken voices.

My wife sat down on the stairs and sobbed. The maid, cursing the revellers, showed them the way to the hotel.

On arriving in Saratov my wife found her mother living with her son and daughter in a room she had rented on the outskirts of town. After her husband's arrest they had been evicted from their flat. There was no news of my wife's brother. Later we learned that by this time he had already perished. A special Commission had sentenced her father to five years in a concentration camp. By selling our things, which she had forwarded from Osipovichi, my wife obtained a little money both for herself and to help me and her father. On more than one occasion she managed to find work but every time, when it was found out after a few days that her husband, her father and her brother were 'enemies of the people,' she was sacked without explanation. All this I found out later, when I was freed.

On May 8th, 1939, after the three-month break in the interrogations, a man came to our cell with a list in his hand and ordered me to get my things ready to leave. My joy knew no bounds. Comrade B., also certain that I was being released, kept on asking me whether I was sure I had not forgotten his wife's address. He begged me to tell her that he was not a scoundrel, that he had just not been able to hold out and had signed the false confession, and that he wanted desperately for her to forgive him; she was to be sure that he loved her. I promised to visit his wife and tell her all that he had passed to me. We embraced and parted.

My step was springy as I walked through the corridors of the prison. I was brought to a halt at a locker and ordered to leave my things there. Then we went on. One of my escorts disappeared through a door to report. After a moment's wait, I was brought into a small hall. I found myself before a court martial. Three men sat at a table. I noticed that the chairman wore a broad golden stripe on the sleeve of his black uniform. 'A captain, first grade,' I thought. My joyful mood did not desert me. This was all I asked for—that a court should try my case.

The proceedings lasted some four or five minutes. My surname, first name, patronymic, year and place of birth were checked. Then the chairman asked: 'Why did you not admit to your crimes during the investigation?'

'I have committed no crimes. I have nothing to confess,' I answered.

'Why then do ten men, who have already been convicted, testify against you?' asked the chairman.

I was in such a good mood at that moment and so certain of my release that I answered in a rather casual way. I later had cause to regret this bitterly.

'I once read a book by Victor Hugo,' I said. 'It tells how in the British Isles in the sixteenth century eleven men were brought to trial for having held communication with the devil. Ten of them confessed—after torture, it's true—but the eleventh did not confess. Then King James ordered the eleventh man to be boiled alive so that it could be proved by his fat that the poor fellow had indeed held communication with the devil. Obviously the ten men who confessed and gave evidence against me went through what those ten

Englishmen went through, and didn't want to experience the fate of the eleventh man.'

The judges laughed and glanced at each other. The chairman, whose name was Nikichenko, asked those sitting beside him: 'Quite clear, isn't it?' They all nodded.

I was taken out into the corridor. Two minutes passed. I was brought back into the hall and the sentence was read out: fifteen years in prison and concentration camp, and five years' deprivation of civil rights.

It was so unexpected I fell to the floor there where I stood.

The same day I was transferred to Butyrki Prison, to a cell in which there were only convicted men awaiting transportation. I greeted them heartily as I went in, and introduced myself military-style.

After Lefortovo this seemed like a rest home. True, there were over seventy prisoners in a cell intended for twenty-five, but every day we were allowed half an hour's walk instead of ten minutes every other day as at Lefortovo. The senior prisoner showed me my place on the edge of the bunk beside the door, next to the latrine bucket. When I had taken up my foot and a half's worth of bunk, my neighbour started: 'How much did you get? Did you sign?'

'Fifteen and five. I signed nothing.'

'Did they use torture?'

'Fully.'

'I've been inside for a long time and in many cells but I've never met anyone who hasn't signed. You're the first here.'

From that moment on they all began to take notice of me.

As prisoners came and went I became an 'old inhabitant,' and moved from the bucket and the door nearer to the window. The senior prisoner of the cell was chosen from among those who had been there a long time. When he was taken away he recommended a successor. His duties were numerous: he supervised the fair distribution of bread, sugar, and other food, sorted out quarrels and separated people who came to blows, though this happened only rarely. He had some measure of responsibility to the prison administration and was in a position to defend the interests of the prisoners to a certain extent.

There were people of various professions and trades in our cell. They were knowledgeable folk and, seated in groups on our bed-planks, we held some interesting conversations. Not one of us knew where he would finish up. The extreme north or east were considered most likely. We therefore listened most attentively to those who had once worked in the remoter regions of the Soviet Union, or whose knowledge of geography was better than ours.

Of the inmates of our cell I was indeed the only one who had not indulged in fantasy and signed a statement concocted by the interrogator. All the rest had incriminated themselves and other people. Some of the stories they had put their names to were extraordinary. One, for example, had admitted that he came from a princely family, that he had survived since 1918 with a passport taken from a peasant he had killed, that during all this time he was sabotaging the Soviet Power, and so on. Many of them, when they heard that I had made no statement, were furious at their own inventions and behaviour. Others consoled themselves by saying: 'It's the same price whether you sign or whether you don't. Gorbatov too has got fifteen and five.' And there were some who just did not believe me.

Then, at long last, most of us were ordered to get ready to leave. We were driven to the railway and put into goods trucks. All were silent, each occupied with his own thoughts. Something still made me believe that truth would triumph and I would be freed.

EIGHT

Kolyma

When we left the Volga behind us it became clear that we were bound for Siberia. In the transit prison at Sverdlovsk we were allowed to buy paper and write letters for the first time. 'Ink only, and nothing unnecessary,' was the order. I wrote to Saratov, to my wife's mother's address, knowing that even if my wife had not returned to her parents they would forward the letter. I told her where I was and that we would probably be moving on in a few days. I begged her not to grieve but to think of herself, and not to come to Sverdlovsk; she would not find me there in any case. Many of our group did write to their relatives asking them to come to Sverdlovsk to see them. A few came and brought food, and saw their wretched kin. It was this very thing that I and others of a like mind had wanted to avoid. We could guess easily enough the distress our relations were in.

My wife got thoroughly depressed when the current instalment of fifty roubles which she had sent to Lefortovo was returned to her. She went to Moscow. At the Enquiry Office of the N.K.V.D. she was informed that, as an un-repentant and recalcitrant criminal, I had been sentenced to twenty years, but that I was allowed to correspond. They told her that when I reached one of the camps in the Maga-dan region I would probably write to her. As she was young and attractive the best they could wish for her was that she would soon marry again. However much she abhorred this

shameless advice she appreciated the word 'unrepentant'—
it told her that I had not signed under the false accusations
made against me. She went to a lawyer, filed a complaint
and had it sent to the Supreme Court. She managed to get
an interview with the Chief Military Prosecutor. He shrugged
his shoulders but approved the submission of the complaint.
When she returned to Saratov she received my letter from
Sverdlovsk written ten days earlier.

This method of communication did not satisfy me. For one
thing, I was convinced that my wife did not know about my
behaviour at the investigation and had no idea that I had
been sent to Kolyma. One of the five common criminals in
our truck had a small pencil stub which he had hidden when
he was searched. This he agreed to sell me for two packets of
makhorka. I sent to a shop for the tobacco and two packets of
cigarette paper. I gave the convict the tobacco, took the
pencil from him and, as the train moved off again, wrote a
letter on the cigarette paper, numbering each sheet. Next I
made an envelope of the *makhorka* wrapper and stuck it
down with moistened bread. So that my letter should not be
carried by the wind into the bushes beside the railway, I
weighted it with a crust of bread which I tied on with threads
pulled from my towel. Between the envelope and the crust
I slipped a rouble note and four cigarette papers each with
the message: 'Would the finder of this envelope please stick
on a stamp and post it.' I sidled up to the window of our
truck just as we were going through a big station and let the
letter drop as we passed over the last set of points. If the
letter was picked up with witnesses around I was afraid that
it would not be sent to its address but would go where I least
wanted it to. Two years later my wife told me that she had
received this letter without either a stamp or a postmark. It

had given her new strength to face life and helped her to battle more stubbornly for my release.

While my wife was going through endless trouble on my behalf, our train was slowly taking us eastward. Our sordid convoy stopped for de-infestation at Novosibirsk, Irkutsk and Chita. I was afraid that while we were at the baths I would be robbed by the common criminals, so I washed myself with my right hand and held my money in my left. But in Irkutsk—I remember it well—we had finished washing and were off to get dressed when one of these convicts brought me down with a back-heel while two others forced open my left hand and took away my money, to the accompaniment of loud laughter from one type of prisoner and gloomy silence from the other. Protests or complaints were useless.

We saw many convoys of troops, artillery, tanks and vehicles on station platforms along our way. We did not know where they were going; we thought maybe war had started with Japan. It occurred to me that if the Japanese pinned down our forces in the east, the Germans would strike from the west. We contrived to connect every event imaginable with our personal fate. Some said that if a war began there would be a shortage of food and we would starve. Others disagreed: experienced fighting men would be needed, and we would go free. Others again were certain that we would not be taken to Kolyma, since the road to it would now be closed. What worried the soldiers among us more than our own circumstances was the question: if a war really had begun, how many unnecessary losses would there be in the forces deprived, as a result of the arrests, of their most experienced commanders?

After Nerchinsk we saw no more military convoys. I thought that the troops were probably moving into Mongolia.

In fact operations had already started at Khalkhin-Gol, but it was only much later that I heard about this.

Finally, at the beginning of June, 1939, we arrived at Vladivostok and were put into wooden huts surrounded by barbed wire, just outside the town. There were many prisoners there already. We were kept there for ten days. It became clear that there was no war with Japan, and that Kolyma was our destination. We were being held up to await the arrival of further convoys of prisoners still on their way. There was a large ship to be filled.

One day I heard a camp orderly shouting: 'Volunteers for work, carrying water to the coppers?' I had been longing for an honest job of work to do and volunteered straight-away, afraid only that someone else might get the job. Fortunately there were no competitors.

Water for the prisoners was boiled in twelve obsolete field kitchens a short distance from the huts, and the stand-pipe was about a hundred yards further on. Finding myself away from the general commotion, out of sight of the gloomy faces and out of hearing of the sighs, I regained my composure, as far as this was possible, straightened my shoulders and set to work with a will. The weather was fine, the sun was shining and a pleasant breeze was blowing. Un-doing the collar of my tunic I let the wind blow on my chest and breathed deeply of the fresh air, thanking the sun and the wind for their kindness to us innocent wretches.

The foreman of the working party at the boilers, a common criminal, noticed how hard I worked, told me he would always call on me in future. I was glad. I liked it there and I worked all out, day and night, returning to the hut only for roll-call and for meals.

One morning a large group of women came for water. We got into conversation and I learned from them that a column of women had arrived, all convicted under Article 58. As Grigorev, the commander of the 7th Cavalry Corps, had been arrested it was not impossible that his wife would be among these women. When I was still free I had been told that a husband would often be arrested first, and later the wife. I asked them whether there was a Maria Andreevna, wife of Corps Commander Grigorev, among them.

'There are so many of us,' said one of the women. 'We don't know whether there's anyone of that name. If we see her what shall we tell her?'

'Tell her to come and fetch water tomorrow morning— Gorbatov, the former divisional commander, wants to see her.'

'All right, we'll look around. We'll ask her if we see her.'

Next morning when the women came for water it was not Grigorev's wife that was among them but his niece, who had been brought up by the Grigorevs from an early age and had married Bzhezovski, the head of the division's Special Department. They had first arrested her husband and shortly afterwards her as well.

'Fancy meeting Aleksandr Vasilevich here!' she said, across the wire fence.

'Yes, Lubochka. I never expected to see you here either,' I said. She had been accused of espionage and convicted. She, too, was on her way to Kolyma.

New people were constantly flooding into our transit camp. Soon we were transported to Nakhodka Bay and put aboard the S.S. *Dzhurma*, bound for Magadan.

An even deeper gloom settled on the prisoners as the shore receded. Until that moment I had never lost hope for a single minute, but now even I was seized at times by the feeling that I was doomed.

We were put in the hold. From time to time we were taken

on deck to get some fresh air. Once during exercise we saw
our ship was passing through the Straits of La Pérouse. To
our right the shore of Japan was visible and to our left the
southern tip of Sakhalin, annexed by the Japanese in 1905.
A strange alarm overcame us and in our excitement we even
spoke more softly. It occurred to me then that if we were
not freed before war with Germany and Japan broke
out, an event which I considered inevitable, we would
never get away in wartime because the Straits would be
closed and the only other escape route—by air—seemed
unthinkable.

The weather was fine as far as the Straits of La Pérouse,
but when we entered the Sea of Okhotsk the storms began
and our huge ship was tossed about like a splinter of wood.
Although I was less affected than the majority of my companions I found the stuffiness unbearable. We were not
allowed on deck because the captain and the commandant
of the convoy were afraid that someone might be washed
overboard. The figures wouldn't tally then, and they would
have to answer for it!

While we were in the Sea of Okhotsk misfortune befell me.
Early in the morning, when I was lying half-awake as many
of us did, two 'trusties' came up to me and dragged away my
boots which I was using as a pillow. One of them hit me hard
on the chest and then on the head and said with a leer:
'Look at him—sells me his boots days ago, pockets the cash,
and then refuses to hand them over!'

Off they went with their loot, laughing for all they were
worth and only stopping to beat me up again when, out of
sheer despair, I followed them and asked for the boots back.
The other 'trusties' watched, roaring with laughter. 'Let him
have it! Quit yelling—they're not your boots now.'

Only one of the political prisoners spoke up: 'Look, what

are you up to? How can he manage in bare feet?' One of the thieves took off his pumps and threw them at me.

I had often heard, since I had been in prison, stories about the bestial behaviour of the common convicts but to be honest I never thought they would rob with such impunity in the presence of other prisoners. Anyhow, I lost my boots. Our guards, including their chief, got on well with the 'trusties,' encouraged them to violence and used them to mock the 'enemies of the people.'

At last we reached Magadan, the chief town of Kolyma. When we had been subjected to a medical examination of sorts and split up into groups, all of us, except for the obviously sick, were sent to distant mines, from three hundred to four hundred miles from the town.

There can be no doubt that the development and exploitation of the Kolyma region was in large measure the work of prisoners—from the time, of course, when the so-called 'enemies of the people' were first sent out there, men highly qualified in a variety of jobs and accustomed to work not out of fear but for the satisfaction of their conscience. Nor can there be any doubt that these people would have done infinitely more if they had not been continually nagged by the thought of their unmerited humiliation, if they had not been tormented by fears for the fate of those dearest to them, if they had lived in conditions fit for human beings, and if their labour had been directed by knowledgeable and conscientious leaders, rather than by foremen drunk with the unlimited power which they had acquired by pure chance.

It will be a long time before the significance of this period in the history of our country has been fully assessed. The aim of my story is to tell the younger generation about people

who even in those conditions did not lose their faith in
justice, in the great Party of Lenin and in our own Soviet
Power, even though many of these unfortunates lost any
hope of every finding freedom again. But there were also
among us people who had lost faith in all that is dearest to
Soviet man and who thought only of how best to save themselves. Their only concern was to find ways of pleasing the
scoundrels, the true enemies of Communism and the Soviet
people. Some of these cowards put a face on their surrender
by a variety of 'philosophies.'

My neighbour on the plank bed in the camp at Kolyma
had once been head of the political department of a railway.
He prided himself on having incriminated some three
hundred people. He said, as I had often heard in prison in
Moscow, 'The worse it is, the better it is—like that it will all
be cleared up more quickly.' He also claimed to see a kind
of 'historical necessity' in the mass arrests; he suggested
parallels from the times of Ivan the Terrible and Peter the
Great. I took no pains to conceal my extreme distaste for this
theory-spinning slanderer.

He was always trying to engage me in conversation. At
first this angered me, but later I began to think that he was
trying to still his conscience by talking to me. On one
occasion, however, he drove me into a rage. 'It is you and
the likes of you,' I told him, 'who have tangled the skein so
that it will be hard to unravel. It will be unravelled, never
you mind, but if I were in your place I would have hanged
myself long ago.' The next morning he was found dangling
from a rope. Though I loathed him his death troubled me
acutely for a long time.

In July, 1939, I found myself at the Maldyak mines,
three hundred and sixty miles from Magadan. The drive
took five days, the first two hundred miles over a highway

cut from the permafrost and the remainder over a dirt track. We passed through hilly country covered with larches, asps, birches and cedars. Whenever we stopped we fell on the ripe cedar cones and stored them away to eat on the road. The forest was out of bounds to us, on pain of death.

The settlement at the Maldyak goldfields consisted of wooden huts, each with at most three windows. The free workers lived in these. In the camp, surrounded by barbed wire, there were ten large double hospital-type tents, each one holding fifty to sixty prisoners. Apart from these there were timber administrative quarters, the mess, the store rooms, the guard house and, beyond the wire, wooden barracks for the guards, together with the mine shafts and two tanks for washing out the ore.

There were about four hundred political prisoners convicted under Article 58 and some fifty 'trusties,' hardened criminals with more than one conviction on their record, and some of them with several apiece, including one with as many as eight robberies with murder. These were the men who were put in charge of us.

The gold-bearing ore was dug at depths of thirty-five to forty metres. The permafrost is a compact aggregate, as hard as granite, on which we used electric miners' picks. The ore was removed in wheelbarrows to a special hoist, and lifted to the trolleys in which it was taken away to be panned.

Our mine was doing well. Several kilogrammes of gold a day were produced and there were days, rare it is true, when as many as ten kilogrammes were obtained. Sometimes sizeable nuggets turned up. I only heard about them and never saw them myself. Three small nuggets were all I found, the largest weighing a hundred and fifty grammes.

Some of the old-timers were real triers. They would go down into the mine with water and a pan to wash the ore and they seldom sifted out less than twenty-five to thirty grammes of gold. I would often watch them inspecting the the sides of the shaft, sometimes with the aid of a pocket torch. When they found a likely spot, these master-craftsmen would hack out the ore and sift it in their pan. Once a man stayed down in the mine for seventy hours. Food and water were brought to him. In that time he sifted out about two kilogrammes of gold.

Work at the goldfield was pretty killing, particularly so considering the bad food we were given. The 'enemies of the people,' as a rule, were detailed for the heaviest jobs, the lighter work being given to the 'trusties' or common criminals. As I have already said, it was they who were appointed foremen, cooks, orderlies and tent seniors. Naturally enough the small amounts of fat released for the pot chiefly found their way into the bellies of the 'trusties.' There were three types of rations: one for those who had not fulfilled their quota, another for those who had, and a third for those who had exceeded their quota. The latter automatically included the 'trusties.' They did little enough work but the tally clerks were of their persuasion and so they swindled, putting to their own and their mates' credit the work that we had done. As a result the criminals fed well and the politicals went hungry.

To keep our tents warm in winter we built walls of snow round them. No limit was set to the amount of fuel we could use in the iron stoves; we were allowed to burn as much as we could fetch from the forest after work. Frosts of forty to fifty degrees centigrade were usual in these parts. Escape would get you nowhere, so there was no particular check on people going outside the wire. You went up to a guard and said 'I'm off for wood,' and you marched unmolested out of the camp.

If you wanted a bit extra above what you were given in the mess, you would take some wood to the owner of one of the huts. This would get you a piece of bread, large or small depending on the size of your bundle. Most of the free miners had come there to turn an honest penny for themselves and so were not particularly generous; no crusts of bread were given away. But undoubtedly there were some good men among them, and anyway we treasured any work they put in our way because it was our only chance of extra food. Most of them had their regular porters and woodcutters, though.

Sometimes it happened that we and the criminals were sent off for wood together. We, the 'enemies of the people,' would go into the forest; the criminals would lie in wait for us not far from the camp. As we came back they would grab our load and, if they were feeling generous, say: 'We'll help you carry that.' We were forbidden to return to camp without any wood and so back we had to go for more, a couple of miles into the forest. Sometimes things went even worse, depending on who happened to come your way. You might be attacked and have your load snatched from you, and you might be badly beaten up, for good measure, and told: 'You're a Communist, aren't you? You defended Soviet Power, didn't you? Well, here's your thanks . . . !'

Soon things started to go badly with me. My legs began to swell and my teeth grew loose in my gums. To lie down sick on the job was bad—there was only ever one result—so I went to see the doctor. He was in fact only a doctor's assistant, sentenced to ten years for some trifle. He was a decent man. He certified me sick, pronounced me fit for light duties only and fixed me up as watchman of the summer water tank. This was considered a privilege; you did not have to push around heavy barrows and trolleys. All you had to do was make sure that no one stole the dry wood for the stoves. I held my rank as watchman for two weeks. I sat in a shelter which I had made out of snow, and kept a small fire going in there. I had a pick and an axe and I used them to hack pieces off tree stumps and drag them into my snow house to keep the fire going.

The work was not hard and inwardly I often thanked the kindly doctor. But my legs went on swelling until they looked like logs and my knees would no longer bend. I had to go back to the doctor. He certified me as completely unfit and wrote a recommendation for my removal from Maldyak to a camp some twelve miles from Magadan. Everything now depended on the camp commander. Fortunately he initialled the document and at the end of March, 1940, I found myself near Magadan. This and only this saved me from certain death. I wish I could remember the name of the doctor at Maldyak. I shall be grateful to him for ever.

When I had first reached Magadan from Vladivostok it had seemed a wild place to me. Now, after Maldyak, Magadan seemed cosy and the air quite different, as if I had gone in November from the north of Russia to Sochi on the Black Sea Coast.

We were housed in a large barrack camp at the foot of the mountains. As we were weak from sickness and the long, hard journey we were not sent to work for four days. Those four days flashed by like a dream. Then we set to work again collecting logs, carrying them on our backs or dragging them on a sledge. Our quota was fifty-four cubic metres of wood per day.

The reader will find it hard to picture a straggling line of men, or rather shadows of men, strung out over three miles as they weave their way along the mountain slope, gaunt, draining their last ounce of strength, their necks stretched forward like cranes in flight as they drag the wood behind them. It is hard enough to pull a load downhill, it is harder still to pull it on the flat, but the slightest slope puts it beyond your strength; you stumble, fall, get up, and fall again, but nothing will shift the load except another man pushing from the back. Somehow we got the wood back to the camp.

The work grew harder every day. In the evenings we would argue among ourselves why this should be so.

'We've all had it, at this rate,' someone would say.

Another would say bitterly: 'It's the spring. We've all been waiting for it. And now it's here it wets the snow and makes it harder to drag the wood. That's why our legs are hurting like this.'

'The rotten food's behind it all,' a third would chip in decidedly. 'It's no better than at Maldyak, and the work's just as hard.'

What were we to do? We couldn't say that we were ill: they would just cut our bread ration. What medicine would they give us, anyway? There was only one medicine to be had—an infusion of pine needles. Beyond that there was only one alternative—six feet under. So pull, comrade, pull while you still can.

During our four days' rest we had each been telling the story of our lives. During my tale Loginov, a highly qualified engineer, asked me: 'Aleksandr Vasilevich, aren't you cursing yourself now for the honest work you've done? Hasn't the result of that mock trial changed your outlook somewhat?'

'No,' I replied. 'If I had to live my life again, I would repeat what I have done, even if I knew that I would be sent to Kolyma. If I were free now I would serve in the army again, even if I had to re-enlist as an extended service man. Besides, why blame the Court? Someone told them to do what they did.'

'I expected no other answer from you,' said Leonid Ignatievich. 'I am like that myself. I'd be a simple worker for the rest of my life if only I were free and people knew I was innocent.'

I dreamed once that an order had come for my immediate release. Everyone else knew about it, but days and weeks went by and I was not told. How I cursed the authorities! When reveille came I was glad it had only been a dream. Otherwise my sentence would certainly have been increased for the language I had used.

One day a shameful thing happened to me. I had received the money which my wife regularly sent me, and decided to buy myself a treat—some tinned fish from one of the 'trusties.' While I was getting the money out of my handkerchief two convicts came up to me, seized the handerchief and the money to roars of laughter from the others, and lost themselves in the crowd of men streaming into the mess hall. I minded less about the money than about the pile of letters from my wife and her photographs, which the scoundrels had snatched out of my hands together with the money. I had read each letter over and over again, and, when alone, had looked at the photographs. I met the malefactors again and asked them to return at least the photographs. They only laughed. When I opened the tin of fish it was full of sand.

Prisoners react in different ways to hard labour. Some, as soon as they touch the planks, go off to sleep straightaway, even though they may sleep restlessly. Others toss and turn from side to side and take a long time to fall asleep. I slept badly. There was no time to think at work but at night, under the dim lights, one could mull things over, the past, the present and the future.

I used to recall Butyrki prison. How I used to dream in those days of being freed, or at least of being sent to a camp to work, where I could breathe fresh air! I had never imagined that there were camps like this. Now, hungry, lying on my hard bed, I dreamed how marvellous it would be to be in prison, even just for a few days—to be able to lie about, rest in the warmth and eat one's fill of bread.

My thoughts often turned to my wife; how hard her life must be, a woman of many sorrows, her father, brother and husband taken at one go. I remembered how we pitied our friends when they had been arrested, never suspecting that our own grief was just at the door.

Most of all I thought about my country's fate. If I, and only I, had been arrested, that would have been my own, private sorrow. But so many of the most devoted, talented and highly skilled men of every kind had been taken—this was a cause for sorrow for the country as a whole. War seemed imminent and inevitable. I wondered how the officers newly appointed to high rank, with no battle experience, would deal with operations in a real war. Honest, brave men devoted to their country they might be, but yesterday's battalion commander would be head of a division, yesterday's regimental commander of a corps; in charge of an army, or a whole front, there would be at best a former divisional commander or his deputy. How many futile losses and failures would there be? What would our country suffer just because of this?

Another problem tormented me. Did our leaders really believe that so many Soviet people had all of a sudden become corrupt and turned to spying for the Imperialists? If this were really so, who was it that had upheld, indeed who was still upholding the Soviet Power? No, it was impossible. But the same cursed question would come to me again: how did it happen? I could find no answer.

There were many criminals in our new camp and, as at Maldyak, they worked little and lived well. For a long time one of these individuals had been pestering me to sell him my woollen tunic. He was the senior in one of the tents and drew the bread ration to distribute to the other prisoners, so that he always had surpluses. One day I received a letter from my wife in which she told me that she had sent a parcel containing a new tunic, trousers, underwear, boots and a dry sausage. I showed this letter to the 'trusty.' 'I can't sell you the tunic I'm wearing, but I will let you have the other one when I get it, provided you supply me with extra bread.'

'All right,' he answered, 'I'll let you have a ration of six hundred grammes a day.' And, to do him justice, he kept his promise.

From long experience, however, I knew that the good things never got as far as me. Up to now I had never received what my wife had told me she had sent. Some parcels simply failed to arrive. So, not being very hopeful of ever seeing the latest parcel, I felt sure that the extra bread, which was keeping me on my feet, would only be available for a limited time. It was a question of planning a lighter job well ahead. With the help of another prisoner, Gorev, who enjoyed a certain amount of authority, being in charge of part of the workshops, I managed to obtain a job splitting firewood and heating water in the boilers. I was up to this work, and it was warm there.

Next to the boilers stood the camp administration sector where a man called Egorov worked as an accountant. He had once been a finance clerk in Yaroslavl. I got to know him and offered to tidy and sweep his office regularly, in the hope that this might bring the extra crust of bread my way. Egorov agreed—he stood to lose nothing—and I congratulated myself as I swept crusts and crumbs and sometimes even little chunks of bread off the tables into my bag. Now I was able to still my hunger to some extent.

Not far from the place where I worked there were a number of clamps which Egorov looked after, in which were kept potatoes, carrots and onions. I also worked that— hunger is no genteel old lady—picking over the vegetables. I could not chew raw potatoes or carrots whole as my teeth were loose, so I made myself a grater by punching holes with a nail in a piece of tin. Now I was eating raw vegetables my teeth began to strengthen and the swelling of my legs went down. I could even help some of my comrades in misfortune, including my friend Loginov.

One day I received a letter from my wife. She told me not to worry about her; she was well and had found an easy and well-paid job as a checker in a factory. She said she had already mastered the work and her workmates and superiors were pleased with her. (I learned later that all this was pure fantasy. She was, in fact, unemployed at that time.) In spite of this, she said, she had decided to come to work at Magadan to be near me; she had already got the promise of a permit.

This terrified me. I wrote her two almost identical letters right then and sent them off with an interval of seven days in the hope that one of them at least would reach her. Delighted that she had found a good job, I objected strongly to her intention of coming to Magadan. Lying in my turn, I told her that I was leaving soon for a distant goldfield. I tried to convince her—and for all practical purposes it was indeed the truth—that she was where I needed her most, near Moscow.

By the time I had finally recovered and regained my

strength, the short Kolyma summer was upon us. Many, both sick and healthy, had longed for my warm job beside the boilers. Now the lists were open for work at the fisheries. I was among the first to volunteer. A week later I said good-bye to my friends and moved to Ola, by the sea. Here I met my old comrade, Fedorov, the former commander of the 28th Cavalry Division, now working at his father's old trade as a blacksmith. We embraced and exchanged news. Life was fairly good in Ola. The regime was less strict, the prisoners could walk about the village freely, and I was able to see a lot of Fedorov.

A few weeks later came the call for volunteers to go into the taiga, to cut hay for a month. I volunteered on the spot. Four of us, myself and three criminals, were given scythes, rakes, whet-stones and enough food for a week: bread, groats and salt, also a tattered fishing net. We stacked the food and equipment on a cart and set off through the forest following the River Ola upstream.

After two days we found a large clearing where the grass was thick and high and we decided to make this our base. We built a hut of branches, covered it with grass that we had scythed, made a pen for the horse not far from the hut, chopped firewood and lit a smoky fire inside the hut to drive away the clouds of midges and mosquitoes. We laid our net in the nearby stream and settled down for the night.

Early next morning I was woken up by the snorting of the horse. 'A gnat's bitten him,' I thought, and fell asleep again. When I went out later I found that three round loaves had vanished from the cart. We had lost three-quarters of our week's bread ration. A trail of flattened grass led from the cart to the edge of the forest. There a large patch of grass was beaten down. Someone had obviously been lying there.

Breadcrumbs were scattered around. 'A runaway prisoner,' was my first thought, but then I saw the fresh droppings of some large animal. I roused my comrades and told them what had happened. We reached the same conclusion—it could only be a prank of Mikhail Ivanovich Toptygin *alias* Misha Flatfoot the bear. My comrades were worried about what we were going to do for food for the rest of the week. But something else worried me. That day Toptygin had eaten a good breakfast. He now had our address. He would certainly return tomorrow. And if he found no bread he might well try the horse, and then our turn would come.

This ruined our mood. But there was nothing to be done about it for the moment, and we had work to do. I went to the stream for water and happened to cast a glance ar the net. To my great joy there were ten fish in it—salmon, the hump-back and the Siberian kind. My shouts brought the others running. Together we pulled the net ashore with its unexpected catch. We took out the fish and put the net back in the stream.

Breakfast was glorious, and uncommonly filling. The fish soup was best, with caviare instead of groats. We did not even think of bread. After our large meal we went to work in a better mood. The weather was sunny and warm and we forgot all about our fearsome neighbour. My job was to cook, look after the horse and find the places for cutting hay, and I kept pretty busy at it.

At dawn the next day the horse woke me again. He was snorting and pawing the ground. Again, with difficulty, I roused my young companions and leapt from the tent. I saw the bear walking along on his hind legs towards the forest. In his front paws he carried our sack of bran, clasped to his chest. He kept looking back at the hut as he hurried away. Then he spotted me. He stopped, turned his muzzle towards me and, very carefully, as if afraid to spill the bran, stood the sack on the ground. It fell over. The bear began to shift uneasily from one foot to the other. I couldn't make out whether he was trying to make excuses for being caught red-handed, or whether he was squaring up to me. My comrades dashed from the hut at my shout. 'Grab the scythes!' I told them. Two of them did, but the third, the youngest, picked up a stone and slung it at the thief. It hit the bear's stomach with a dull thud. He seemed to take offence, because he turned about, got down on all fours and slowly ambled off into the forest, glancing over his shoulder at us as he went. We were about to turn on the stone-thrower but he said: 'Who knows what might have happened if I hadn't hit him with that stone?' So ended our first meeting with Toptygin.

That same day I was fortunate enough to see his wife and children. I had prepared a fish dinner and thought it would be a treat to have some of the bilberries which grew in great numbers in the forest. On my way to pick them I suddenly saw, some two hundred yards away, the bear's mate splashing in a stream with her son or daughter. Another one of her offspring sat on the bank screwing up his eyes at the bright sun. The bear hoisted one cub out of the water, pushed the other one in with her snout and began to wash him. Then they all sat down on the bank to dry off. Suddenly, the mother raised her muzzle, sniffed the wind and looked round. The whole family rose and walked off quietly into the forest. I was watching from behind some bushes, my fear entirely gone. I was only sorry that my comrades had missed this family idyll.

My third meeting with a bear happened on our fourth day. I was walking through the forest in search of new clearings to mow, bending down every now and then to pick bilberries, when I heard the crack of a twig. Straightening up I saw to my horror, a hundred yards or so away and walking towards me, a bear very like my old acquaintance. He saw me and stopped. I confess I was shaking with fright. He had probably recognised me, too. But he was obviously at home here and felt master of the situation. He stood still for a little while and then walked off. Perhaps, sensing my fear, he had decided to leave it at that and show that he had no evil designs on me.

An odd thought struck me then. This powerful beast had shown a generosity that had been clearly lacking in many of the worthless people who had crossed my path in the last two years.

Our forest hosts did not visit us at the camp again.

Of the three convicts who were working with me two were old recidivists but the third was still quite young, no more than twenty-two. The day's work finished, we would sit around in the hut, feeding the fire with logs and chatting about whatever came into our heads.

Alexei, nicknamed 'Stumpy,' was the eldest. He was short, broad-shouldered and powerful. High cheek-bones stood out in his ugly face, and he had three fingers missing from his left hand. He was generally morose and taciturn but once, not without great difficulty, he managed to get out: 'I've done two big jobs myself. One was with one murder. The second one I did three people in.' I asked him how he had lost his fingers. He laughed and glanced at his comrades.

'Go on, tell him, Alexei,' said the youngest. 'We can stand hearing it again.'

'All right, I'll tell him. I lost my fingers at a camp. Not at Kolyma—earlier. I was playing cards and I lost. I had no cash so I staked a good suit, not mine of course, one that a political had on. I lost. I meant to take the suit during the night when the new prisoner had stripped for bed. I had to hand it over before eight in the morning, only they took the political away to another camp that very day. Our council of seniors met to hand out my punishment. The plaintiff wanted all my left hand fingers off. The seniors offered two. They bargained a bit and agreed on three. So I put my hand on the table and the man I'd lost to took a stick and with five strokes knocked off my three fingers.'

Stumpy was quite cool about his story. He added: 'We have our laws too, only tougher than yours. If you do your comrades down you've got to answer for it.'

The second convict, Boris, was nicknamed 'the Careerist.' He got this name in one of the northern camps because he made himself out to be a big criminal, with six murders and five major robberies to his credit. He was believed, and was appointed a senior prisoner. Then it turned out that he was simply an independent, small-time thief. There was a great fuss and he was demoted and given his nickname.

The third one, the youngest, was named Vasya. He had not yet earned himself a nickname. He had lost his mother when he was two, and his father had been hanged by the Whites in the Ukraine. An aunt had brought him up. He ran away from her, became a homeless waif and fell in with 'people like these here'—he indicated the 'trusties' sitting beside him. With them he had robbed a savings bank. One of them was caught straight away, the others later. The Court gave them twelve years in Kolyma.

'It all happened,' explained Vasya, 'because I had no parents and because I ran away from my aunt.'

He cursed himself and deeply repented of all he had done. I was sorry for Vasya and believed him to be sincere. He was a good worker. He used to call me 'Dad.' When we were alone I tried to convince him that if he could preserve his self-respect in the camp he would be able to settle down after his release and lead a happy life. I tried to shield him from the influence of Stumpy and the Careerist. I used to tell him how great and just and humane was our Party. He asked me once: 'Then how did you get here, Dad?'

'Bad people invented things about me,' I answered. He understood this, and believed me.

One day the bunch of them, and Vasya in particular, asked me to tell them about myself, about my childhood, my youth, and my military service. They liked what I told them and asked me to go on, missing out no details. They listened with interest, asking many questions, and afterwards heatedly argued about the way I and other people had behaved. Vasya said sadly how fine it was to grow up in a family, to have parents, even if you were poor and your father was stern. Strangely enough the Careerist agreed with him more often than not. Stumpy rarely joined in, but when we were talking of my childhood, he muttered 'I'd have dealt with a father like that . . . working so much and living like that . . . no, I'd rather be in jail.'

My listeners were particularly taken with my account of how I first fell in love, and parted for ever of my own accord from the girl whom I loved, and who loved me. Vasya and the Careerist expressed surprise at my relationship with Olya but approved my action. Only Stumpy hissed between his teeth: 'Well—that's beyond me all right. The way I look at it, it may take an hour or so but I get it.'

But I noticed that even Stumpy's eyes seemed to soften and become warmer during my story. When I had told them everything up to my arrest, he suddenly said: 'Maybe even I would have agreed to take on your life, Aleksandr Vasilevich.'

At the end of the third week we were brought fresh stores—

bread, groats, salt and bran. The prisoner who brought them checked our work and praised it, jotted everything down and told us our task for the following week. Unfortunately the bread he had brought turned out to be sodden and inedible. We were indignant and pressed him to take it back and show it to someone in authority. The man took me aside, explained the situation at the camp, and said: 'It's not surprising, those three getting steamed up, they're in the clear. But you're an Article 58 man. If you protest they might take it as insubordination and incitement. That would cost you another five years or even ten. I can see for myself the bread's unusable, but that's all you'll get this time so you'll just have to wait a week anyhow whether you like it or not. Why don't you keep it—that would be better—instead of making me take it back. It would be dangerous for me—I'm in the same boat as you.'

But my comrades would not keep the bread and uttered all manner of oaths. Finally, the prisoner who had brought up the stores had to take back the bread. We gave him four large fishes for a present.

I worried for five days about what would happen to us on account of the bread, and passed on my fears to the other three.

'What's that to do with us?' said one of the convicts—I don't remember which—'It was the divisional commander who didn't like the bread. We didn't mind. We've had far worse.'

Only then did I realise the full seriousness of the carter's warnings.

We fed every day on excellent fresh fish. It was the time of year when the two kinds of salmon came up the rivers and tributaries from the sea to spawn. We even stopped eating the hump-back kind, keeping only the caviare. The Siberian salmon we turned into fish soup.

One day, after a good dinner, we went off to cut hay and saw our old friend Misha once more. He was leaning with his front paws on the steep bank of a brook, staring intently into the water.

'He's probably getting ready for a date,' I joked. 'He's using the water as a mirror.' But the bear plunged in and began to splash about in the water.

'No, she's obviously been unfaithful, or else she doesn't like his face,' said Vasya, 'so he's decided to drown himself.' We went on watching, hidden among the bushes.

Misha waded upstream and emerged on his hind legs where the bank was less steep. In his front paws he held a large quivering fish. He sat down, made a snack of it, and vanished into the forest through which we had to pass. We didn't know how far he had gone, nor did we know his mood, so we decided to call it a day and have a rest after dinner to give him time to get out of the way. That was my last meeting with the forest landlord.

We were getting on well with the hay-cutting. The stacks of dry, sweet-smelling hay were growing higher and higher. The weather was fine, and altogether we felt as if we were at a seaside resort having a good holiday. But the bread which we had sent back kept nagging at me.

Then, well off schedule, in the middle of the week, a cart came to us. A driver I did not know passed me an order from the camp commander: 'Gorbatov is to return immediately.'

'Why?'

He had no idea.

NINE

Reinstatement

I took leave of my workmates, wishing them a reduced prison term and an honest life in the future. Vasya said goodbye to me as though I were his real father and promised to do everything that I had advised him. I felt apprehensive as we set off back to the camp. The lumberjacks we met in the forest could tell me nothing new. In the morning we floated down-river on a raft to Ola.

Before all else I went to see my friend Fedorov and told him about the bread. I asked his opinion about my recall. He had heard nothing. 'But,' he added, 'I think you're in a bad way.'

Still more alarmed, I went to the camp commander. To my surprise he received me well. At first our conversation was right off the point. He asked me how the hay-cutting had gone. I reported and he was pleased with our work. Then he asked with a grin whether I knew the reason for my return to camp. I itched to say that I knew it well enough, but answered firmly: 'No, I don't know.'

'You used to command a division, your name is Gorbatov, Aleksandr Vasilevich, and you are serving fifteen years plus five?'

I replied in the affirmative.

He said: 'You are summoned to Moscow for a review of your case.'

'You are serious? You are not joking?'

For the first time throughout this whole agonising period

someone in authority had used *vy*, the polite form of address, to me, and this alone was a sure sign that the camp commander was not joking.

'Yes, I am serious. And I am glad for you.'

'I am most grateful to you, Comrade Commander, for such pleasant news. I have been expecting it for a long time.'

'People are accustomed to regard men in my position as some sort of fiend. That is a mistake. We also like to bring good news to a prisoner. Unfortunately, it happens rarely.' As we parted, he added: 'You must be ready tomorrow morning to set off for Magadan in the launch. My advice to you is to watch what you say and do until you are in Moscow.' As I left, he shook my hand.

I went straight to Fedorov to tell him my good news. On the way I met the driver who had brought up the stores, including the bread that we would not accept. He asked why I had come back so early from the hay-making. I told him what had happened. 'How lucky I didn't take your bread back to the camp! I fed some to the horses and threw the rest away. You never know—it might have spoilt your good mood.' I flung my arms round him, but could say nothing.

It was not easy to bid farewell to Fedorov and my other comrades who were staying behind. We all wept bitterly, but my tears were bitter for them, joyful for myself. They all asked me to 'say in Moscow' that they were not guilty of anything and in no sense enemies of their own state. 'But who will pay any attention to me?' I asked them helplessly. As the launch moved away I could see them for a long time on the shore, waving their arms.

Later I learned that my wife had never stopped haunting the offices of the N.K.V.D. and of the Attorney-General, the Supreme Court and the People's Commissariat of Defence. Finally, on March 20th, 1940, she had received a letter under the stamp of the Supreme Court. For a long time she could not make up her mind to open it. When she did she burst into tears: she was informed that the Plenum of the Supreme Court had rescinded my sentence and proposed to review my case. At the Plenum S. M. Budienny had played a major part in my defence by affirming that he knew me to be an honest commander and a good Communist; I learned this later from a military prosecutor who had been present at the Plenum. My wife had written to me several times about the Supreme Court's decision, but some of the letters failed to reach me altogether, and the remainder had the relevant passages blacked out by the censor.

It was a long journey to Moscow. I left the settlement at Ola on August 20th, 1940, and did not arrive at the Butyrki Prison in Moscow until December 25th. We were held up at Magadan, and there were wearisome delays at Nakhodka Bay and at the transit camps in Khabarovsk, Chita, Irkutsk, Novosibirsk and Sverdlovsk. At every stop on the journey I sent my wife a letter. I had absolute faith in the favourable outcome of my case. This faith was unshakable, even when at the transit camps I met many who were returning to concentration camps after their cases had been reviewed.

About a hundred of us gathered in Magadan, all with cases for review. We were still put to work, though at less heavy labour. Afraid of falling ill and being left behind when the time came for sailing on the last run before winter set in, we tried to save our strength by taking advantage of our privileges as 'convicts under review.' As far as we could we tried to avoid work altogether.

Eventually we cast off from this mournful shore in the same S.S. *Dzhurma* which had brought us there. As before, there were storms in the Sea of Okhotsk and we had the same unpleasant time as the ship rolled and pitched. But discipline was not so strict for us now. We were often allowed out on deck. Our happiness showed in everything we did—in our movements and our words, in our joy at the fresh wind, the far-off land, even the huge waves. We all seemed to grow and look younger.

Again we passed through the Straits of La Pérouse, but our impressions now were very different from the first time. Now we were sailing west to freedom.

At Nakhodka Bay we triumphantly stepped off the steamer on to the Big Land, as we used to call it, although for us it consisted merely of some wooden huts. That same day, as I went to fetch boiling water, I met Ushakov, former commander of the 9th Division. We flung our arms around each other and, of course, wept. Ushakov had once been thought a man of culture, the best of the divisional commanders. Here he was a foreman in charge of nine camp kitchens, and still considered himself fortunate to have such 'privileged' work.

Ushakov never reached Kolyma, because of his health. An old soldier, he had been wounded eighteen times fighting the Basmachi in Central Asia. He had received four medals for his military service. While we were at Nakhodka Bay Ushakov's fate, for no apparent reason, took a turn for the worse; he was demoted from foreman and put on heavy physical labour.

As I have said, those who were returning to have their cases reviewed enjoyed certain privileges and could move about the camp more freely. One evening I attended a camp concert given by the women prisoners. The performance of one forty-five-year-old former first secretary of a district party committee is etched into my mind. She sang 'Katiusha'—a popular song. It was less a song than a cry of utter despair, the sorrow of a tormented soul. I could not restrain my tears. I wish I knew her name and whether she is alive today. Over twenty-three years have gone by since then, but that song still rings in my ears. I can see even now that primitive stage of bare boards, and the woman standing there in her padded jacket and tarpaulin boots.

I looked at the audience. These were our mothers, wives, sisters and daughters, more often than not convicted merely as members of the families of 'enemies of the people.' If we were not aware of any guilt we had at least been subjected to an accusation; but these unfortunates were simply the victims of arbitrary and blatant cruelty.

The day before our departure from Nakhodka Bay I found Kostya Ushakov in a trench which he was digging. Short, thin and frail, he sat with his head bent over the handle of his spade. When he heard that I was leaving the next day he asked me to 'say back there, in Moscow,' that he had done nothing wrong and had never been an 'enemy of the people.' We again embraced, and parted for ever. Of course I carried out his request and spoke about him wherever I could, until I learned later that he had died shortly after our meeting.

The journey from Nakhodka Bay to Moscow seemed endless. This time we travelled in a prison train with compartments, not in a goods truck. It goes without saying that we had no seats allocated. There were six racks for thirteen people. We rested by turns, in strict rotation—one at a time on each of the four higher racks while nine sat on the lower two. Through a small barred window we would look out to freedom.

I will not conceal the fact that I looked somewhat unprepossessing. I had lost a lot of weight: I measured five feet ten, but weighed only ten stone at that time. The only evidence that I was a soldier was the tunic that had served

me so faithfully over the years, but because of the dirt and
patches it was difficult to determine what its original colour
had been. My quilt trousers were patched, my legs were
wrapped in cloths and I wore miner's ankle boots. I also
had a padded jerkin which was smooth and shiny with dirt,
and on my head I wore a tattered, filthy cap with earflaps.
As I thought of my outward appearance I could only console
myself with the hope that I had preserved my high spirits,
and perhaps developed even further my will-power and
strength of mind.

I had a sack with me, which served chiefly to hide from
predatory eyes a scrap of blanket from which I was never
parted, but I also kept in it some underwear and my iron
reserve for times of sickness: a dozen small biscuits and five
chips from a sugar cane. This was the condition in which
we arrived at Moscow station and were lodged in Butyrki
Prison, which was already familiar to us.

There were forty in our cell. All had come from various
camps and prisons to have their cases reviewed. Some had
already completed the process and half of these were returning to their camps and prisons, but this did not frighten me.
Contrary to all that I heard I believed that not having
incriminated either myself or others would be to my
advantage.

Seven days later I was called before the interrogator. The
documents of my case lay before him, with my old identity
card photograph. When he saw me he burst into laughter.
Then, abruptly, he grew serious. He spent a long time
looking at me and the photograph in turn, then asked me to
walk up and down the room, and finally sat down and told
me to sit opposite him. He asked me my date of birth, who
had been the district commanders when I was serving in
Central Asia and in the Ukraine, who had been corps

commander and so on. Then the investigation began.

One after the other he put forward a whole series of accusations and checked my answers against some other evidence. All this was done quite politely, but he gave me no reason to think that it was leading to my release. So it went on until March 1st, when I was transferred from Butyrki Prison to the inner prison in the Lubyanka.

On the evening of March 4th I was informed that the investigation had been completed, and that I would be released that night. The interrogator asked whether I had any friends in Moscow with whom my wife might have been staying.

'I have,' I answered.

'What do you think, would she have left a uniform there for you?'

'My wife believes that I shall be released. It's possible that she has brought my uniform and left it there.' I told him the telephone number of my friends' house.

The interrogator left the room. When he returned he said: 'Your wife hasn't left anything, and we can't let you out looking like that, even at night.'

I asked him to tell me what he had said over the telephone. When he had told me I said: 'Naturally the answer to the question as you phrased it was "No." Go back and tell them that you are releasing Gorbatov but that he has no clothes to wear. Then, perhaps, you will get a different reply.'

He left again, and this time came back with the answer one might have expected. He drove down himself to see my friends and brought back a full uniform.

At two o'clock on the morning of March 5th, 1941, the interrogator took me in his car to my friends' house in

Komsomolsky Square. When we got there he politely took his leave. 'Here is my telephone number,' he said. 'If anything happens, ring me at any time. You can count on my help.'

As a souvenir I have kept my sack with its rags, my boots and the sugar and biscuits, which were as black as soot after the journey.

We did not go to bed till dawn. I told them where I had been and what I had seen. For reasons which were well understood at that time I could not tell them a hundredth part of what I am writing now. When I left the Lubyanka I had signed a promise to be silent.

I breakfasted and sent my wife a telegram informing her that I had returned from a long and distant posting, and asking her to come to Moscow quickly. Then I called on the People's Commissar of Defence.

My meeting with Marshal of the Soviet Union S. K. Timoshenko was very cordial. I reported my return from 'a long and dangerous mission.'

'I am pleased to see you alive, Aleksandr Vasilevich. As for your health, you'll get that back. Have a rest, get better, and then there's work for you. I have already given the order that you should be reinstated in the army and that you should receive back pay in your old rank for the full thirty months.'

I thanked him from the heart and left his office. I wanted to share my happiness with everyone, but my wife was ill and was expecting me in Saratov. When I arrived she began to recover as if by magic, and within eight days we were back in Moscow. There we were given passes to stay at the Arkhangelskoe Rest House near the city. A month later we left it to continue treatment and rest in Kislovodsk.

We returned to Moscow gay, full of life, and in much

better health. I was a different person when the People's
Commissar saw me again.

'Do you need any more holiday?' he asked.

'No,' I replied.

'Would you like to go back to the cavalry, or would it be
wiser to chose another arm?'

'Not the cavalry again. I would join a rifle corps with
great pleasure.'

'Take deputy commander of a rifle corps for the time
being, so that you can look around and get to know all the
innovations. Later, we'll see . . .'

The People's Commissar described to me the complicated
international situation. 'It looks as though this is the lull
just before the war. We will have to work flat out,' he said as
I left, and he wished me success in my work. That day I
received instructions to join the 25th Rifle Corps in the
Ukraine. My wife and I parted, for a short time it seemed,
but we had a feeling that we were to be parted again for
many years.

I studied our divisions. They were up to strength but I
felt that there was no real co-ordination between them;
their general standard seemed to me poor. The more I
looked into it, the more convinced I became that they
lacked the necessary order, organisation and military
discipline. What was worse was that many of the commanders did not see these failings. Returning to headquarters,
I reported what I had seen, without exaggeration, but
clearly and precisely, to the corps commander. He agreed
with everything I said. But there was no time to make good—
war was in the air.

Everyone was expecting it and few of us soldiers still
nursed the hope that it might be avoided. Yet when the

announcement came that enemy aircraft had attacked Zhitomir, Sevastopol, Kaunas and Minsk, as well as many railway junctions and airfields, and that enemy divisions had crossed our frontier, the news caught everyone by surprise. This in itself was proof of inadequate political preparation in the army.

My own first thought was how fortunate I was to be free, and to have regained my strength. My second thought, however, was for my wife; what a blow this would be to her. Would I ever see her again? I spoke to her over the telephone and heard her voice. In spite of her own grief she tried to cheer me up: the worst was behind us; she had been happy these last three months; she now had the strength to wait for the day of victory.

Part Four

TEN

The Patriotic War

The divisions spent the first two days of the war getting themselves into fighting condition. There was nothing good in the news bulletins. On June 25th we heard that the enemy had occupied Kaunas and Vilnyas. Refugees appeared on the east bank of the Dnieper—whole villages fleeing from the Western Ukraine. We reckoned that the enemy was moving forward quickly because the attack had been sudden, and because Germany had brought under her control the industry of almost the whole of Europe. Of course, that was so. But my earlier fears still made my hair stand on end: how were we going to be able to fight when we had lost so many experienced commanders even before the war had started? Undoubtedly that was one of the main causes of our failures, although no one talked about it. Some even pretended that 'purging the army of traitors' in 1937 and 1938 had increased its strength.

The divisions of our corps were at first concentrated in the forests near Kiev, but when Minsk was lost we returned to the eastern bank of the Dnieper and entrained at Darnitsa and Brovara for transfer to the Western Front. I travelled in one of the trains and at the stops went from carriage to carriage telling the troops how twenty-seven years ago I had gone to war for the first time, firm in the belief that not only would I not be killed but that I would not even be wounded. In 1915, in the second year of the war, the Russian army had had almost nothing of its own: our saddles were Canadian, our boots American, our rifles Japanese, and there was not even enough of this imported stuff, but we fought well. Now we had our own Soviet arms as a result of the industrialisation of the country and it would be shameful if, defending our own Workers' and Peasants' State, we were to fight worse than Russian soldiers had fought before.

When I learned from the officers that many of the men had been brought up from reserve and were not familiar with the new weapons I ordered that they should have training sessions *en route*, at the prolonged stops of which there were several on our journey. We even organised training with live ammunition.

There were observers and machine-guns mounted at the front and rear of the train, but every time even a single enemy aircraft was sighted the train stopped and everyone without special duties climbed out and scattered into the fields. When the aircraft had gone the bugler would play the recall and the soldiers, without hurrying, would return to their carriages. I saw this as a sign of both extreme timidity and poor discipline: the officers were ill-prepared to take command of their sections, and the Party educational work was lacking in forcefulness and zest.

Our train was held up for several hours at Smolensk. Crossing the tracks I met the commander of the 19th Army, Lieutenant-General I. S. Konev. I introduced myself to him and reported the arrival of my train. Looking at me carefully, Ivan Stepanovich suddenly seemed to remember something: 'I think we were neighbours in a sanatorium at Sochi in 1935?' When I told him that this was so he added: 'You've got much thinner since then.' I replied that I had not yet managed to get completely fit again. 'It's good to meet an old soldier at the front, even one I don't know particularly well,' said the general. 'That doesn't happen so often now.'

He told me briefly about the situation on the Western Front, warned me that Vitebsk had already been taken by the enemy, and ordered me to take as much care of the Vitebsk area as I would of my own eyes. He wished me luck and we parted. After my meeting with Konev I found myself plunged in thought. Why was it that, while those who had been commanding regiments in 1936 and 1937 were now in command of armies, or had become deputy-commanders of fronts, and those who before had been in charge of divisions were now commanding whole fronts, I. S. Konev, one of our most experienced commanders, who had commanded a rifle corps as far back as 1935, was now merely in charge of an army?

The trains carrying the 25th Rifle Corps unloaded the troops south-east of Vitebsk. Without waiting for divisions to form up—let alone the entire corps—regiments and even battalions took up positions as soon as they were off the train and went into action some forty miles from Vitebsk.

In that period of the war, particularly in the first month, you often used to hear people saying: 'We've been out-flanked,' 'We're surrounded,' 'Airborne troops have landed in our rear,' and so on. Not only private soldiers but even some of the officers who had not previously been under fire were much too ready to accept such rumours, so common in modern warfare. One morning I heard firing some way off towards Vitebsk. I drew the corps commander's attention to it and got his permission to go and find out what was happening. Along the road I began to meet small groups of soldiers wandering wearily towards the east. When I asked them where and why they were going and got only confused answers, I ordered them to turn back and went on myself. I kept seeing more and more troops going east, and had to stop

more and more often. I told them they ought to be ashamed
of themselves and ordered them to return. I began to feel that
something had gone extremely wrong and that it was now
urgent that I find the regimental commander. I was tired
of stopping and questioning soldiers. I wanted to know as
quickly as possible what had happened. But when I had
driven to within about three miles of the front, I saw the
300th Regiment coming down the road in a general, disorderly retreat. Among the flood of soldiers there were some
shamefaced officers of various ranks. From time to time
enemy shells exploded harmlessly in the fields. Getting out of
my car I shouted 'Halt! Halt! Halt!' When everyone had
stopped I gave the order: 'About turn, everyone!' Having got
everyone back facing the enemy I made them lie down. Then
I gathered the officers together. I tried to find out the reason
for the retreat. Some said they had received an order, handed
down the line. Others said: 'We saw everyone else retreating
and so we began to retreat as well.' From among the soldiers
lying nearby a voice said: 'Just look at the fire the Germans
are putting down while our artillery doesn't do a thing.'
Other voices supported this. It became clear to me that one
reason for the retreat was the effect of artillery fire on men
not accustomed to war, and another was the passing on of an
order which had not originated with the senior command.
But the basic reason was the weakness of the officers who had
not been able to stop the panic and had themselves given way
to the disgrace of a retreat. I explained all this to the officers
in a few words and told them: 'Now dig yourselves in along
this line!'

I asked one of the battalion commanders where the C.O.
of the regiment was. It turned out that in the morning the
C.O. had been about two miles away, towards Vitebsk on the
left-hand side of the road, but no one had seen him since. I

drove for another mile and continued on foot. I scanned the terrain to right and left but could see no one. Finally I heard a shout and saw a soldier running towards me. This was the commanding officer of the 501st Rifle Regiment, one Koste-vich. From a small fox-hole nearby there emerged the regi-ment's chief of staff and a signals corporal. 'How do you come to be in such a position?' I asked the C.O. He replied with a helpless wave of his hand: 'I fully appreciate the gravity of what has occurred but there was nothing I could do; so we decided to stay and die here, rather than retreat without an order.' He wore two Orders of the Red Banner, but he had only recently been called up from the Reserve after spending many years out of the army. I said to him that though he was perfectly capable of dying without leaving his post, what possible use was this to anyone? It embarrassed me to look at his pitiful face.

Clearly there was no point in even thinking of returning the regiment to its former position and so I asked the officers to follow me, put them in my car and drove back to the regiment. I showed Kostevich a place for his observation point, and suggested dispositions for the battalions and their fire support. I ordered him to sort out his sub-units and to establish contact with the observation points of his battalions.

In the forest to the right of the road, I found the corps artillery regiment and discovered that it had not yet got its guns into position, and that the regimental, troop and battery commanders had not even established observation points. I gathered the gunners together, rebuked them, gave the neces-sary orders and put the officers of the artillery regiment in contact with Kostevich. I told them to co-operate. I told Kostevich to send a platoon from each battalion to man the line they were originally intended to hold, and I told the artillery commander to give covering fire.

On my return I gave a detailed report to the corps commander, but saw that this produced no more impression on him than if he had been listening to a report about the successful unloading of the next train. I asked the commander of the 162nd Rifle Division whether he knew what had happened to the 501st Rifle Regiment under his command. He did not know. I had to point out to him the peculiarity of a situation in which I had to report to him about units under his command and not the other way around. I rang up the corps artillery commander to ask him where his artillery regiment was and what it was doing.

'The regiment is in firing positions in support of the 501st Regiment of the 162nd Rifle Division in the Vitebsk area,' he replied firmly.

'Are you sure about that?'

'Yes, well, that is what has been reported to me,' he answered, misgiving creeping into his voice.

'You should be thoroughly ashamed of yourself. You do not know where a regiment directly under your command is located, to say nothing of the fact that you have no idea how the artillery regiments are carrying out their duties. It is your job to control the work of all the artillery in the corps.'

The corps commander was present but took no part in the conversation. At 1300 hours I again heard firing from the same direction. I telephoned the commander of the 162nd Rifle Division and asked him whether he had heard the firing and, if he had heard it, why had he not gone to the 501st Rifle Regiment? 'Don't reply now,' I said. 'Report to me on the road covered by the 501st Rifle Regiment. I'm going out there myself.' I put the phone down.

This time there was no sign of men retreating along the highway, although shells were bursting all along the regiment's line. I began to allow myself some hope that the regiment had been brought under control, and thought: 'It seems you don't need to do much to get a regiment to defend itself!' However, when the divisional commander and I carefully examined the area we could find no trace of the regiment anywhere. The divisional commander made two suggestions: either the regiment was, perhaps, superbly camouflaged, or it had taken up its previous positions two miles further on. We decided to leave our cars on the road and go across the fields to a sparse birch copse. After about half a mile, as we began to climb a small mound, three shots rang out behind us and bullets whistled past our heads.

'Probably one of our rear covering positions,' said my orderly officer. 'They think we want to surrender and so have opened fire on us.'

We turned back and walked towards the source of the shots. As on the last occasion some hours earlier, there emerged from a fox-hole to meet us Regimental Commander Kostevich, and behind him his faithful chief of staff and his corporal.

'That was us shooting,' said the regimental commander, somewhat embarrassed. 'We didn't know it was you.'

He reported that the regiment had withdrawn again as soon as the bombardment had begun—'But they didn't go by the road this time, they went down through that hollow into the woods.' Kostevich mumbled some inaudible excuses to the effect that he hadn't been able to force his regiment to obey his orders. This time I left him where he was and promised to return to him all the men that we managed to catch up with.

In the hollow we saw a broad track through the high, thick grass—the trail of the retreating soldiers. We had gone barely three hundred paces when we saw about a dozen of them sitting round a bonfire drying out their puttees. Four of them had no weapons. I decided that the divisional commander should take this group back to Kostevich, and should then bring up and put under Kostevich's command part of the divisional reserve so as to cover the road. My orderly officer and I went on to collect the rest of the men who had abandoned their positions.

Soon we began to catch up with scattered groups moving east towards the villages of Liozno and Rudnya. We stopped them. I shamed them, I cursed them, I ordered them to return and I watched them as they unwillingly set off, and went on to catch the next lot. I had better admit that in a number of cases, when we drew level with the head of a large group, I got out of my car and ordered the leaders to dismount. Sometimes, I am ashamed to say, I even overstepped what is permissible in dealing with some of the most senior of them. I was very angry with myself later, but there are times when words lose their power.

I hardly closed my eyes that night remembering the way in which the 501st Regiment had retreated from its positions. This was a very large regiment and I had no doubt that the great majority of the men were patriots. Why then had both officers and soldiers retreated; why had no one stayed to defend the position, except for that unfortunate trio? No doubt the regimental commander had been at fault in allowing his men to become so disorganised, but my thoughts led me further. Why had the divisional commander, when he heard the gunfire in the area of the 501st Rifle Regiment, not gone out to the regiment? He was closer to them than I was, and must have heard the guns better than I did. Why, at least, had he not gone out to the regiment immediately I told him of the dreadful things that were going on, instead of waiting till I drove out myself and ordered him to meet me on the road? Was it thoughtlessness or total indifference?

Moreover, what about the officers of the corps artillery regiment? They knew the speed with which the enemy had advanced over the last few days, but when they were a mere six miles from him they had disposed their men as though they were at a rest camp, in a pine grove, with neither a command nor an observation post. Even when the head-quarters of the artillery regiment had seen the disorderly withdrawal of the riflemen, even when they had seen the enemy shells bursting in the fields around them, they had not reacted in the slightest way to what was going on.

To me, newly back in the army, this all seemed an evil dream. I could not believe my eyes. I kept trying to fight back the persistent thought: 'Surely 1937 and 1938 have not so disrupted the soldiers' faith in their officers that they now think they are being commanded by enemies of the people? That cannot be. More likely the reason is that inexperienced officers, who have never before been under fire, are coping timidly and inadequately with vital jobs.' The thought gave me no rest. I decided to speak frankly with the corps commander in the morning in the presence of the head of the political department. This conversation took place, but it produced no results. Events developed too quickly.

In order to prevent the enemy breaking through to our rear and capturing the town of Demidov and the road junction twenty-five miles from the centre of our corps, it was decided to send one rifle regiment with an artillery troop to hold Demidov. Two hours before dark the corps commander sent me to help these troops to organise the defences. I reached the town inside an hour, but neither the regiment nor the troop of artillery had arrived. I found a depleted reconnaissance battalion. There was a possibility that the enemy would reach Demidov before nightfall and I told the C.O. to organise the defence of the western outskirts of the town, to send out motorised reconnaissance in that direction and to be on the alert until our regiment arrived. By this time it was already dark and there was still no sign of the regiment and the artillery. I decided to wait for them and spent the night in a house right on the eastern outskirts of town.

At dawn I was awakened by machine-gun and artillery fire. Motor vehicles roared past me. The commander of the reconnaissance battalion told me that our regiment had still not come, but that enemy tanks and infantry had already penetrated into the town. True enough, three tanks appeared five hundred yards from us and began to fire down the street. We left the town and moved into positions in outlying houses on a hill a mile and a half back. Within the hour a dense wave of infantry emerged from the town, accompanied by fifteen tanks firing as they moved. We were forced to withdraw along the road to Dukhovishchina.

There I discovered that the commander of the western sector and his staff were located in the forests near Yartsevo, about fifteen miles to the south-east. My report that the enemy was some twenty or twenty-five miles from his headquarters was a surprise for Marshal Timoshenko. I was given sixty men from the headquarters guard, six trucks and four quadruple anti-aircraft machine-guns. I was ordered to go to Dukhovishchina and cover, as far as I could, the road to Yartsevo. While withdrawing I was ordered to hold Yartsevo and the road junction, taking under my command all the artillery in the area and all units withdrawing from the front.

I shall never forget those four days spent near Yartsevo. For if each day was alike, filled with violent and unsuccessful

attacks by the enemy, each day was also individually marked
for me by different events.

What I particularly remember of our defences on the first
day is that the artillery observation points set up on the hills
were not even covered by riflemen—I only had the sixty men.
On the second day we were able to make up ten companies
and two battalions from the retreating troops. Our defence
of this sector almost began to look organised. As I had no
communications of my own, I had to use those of the artillery.
I fully made up for this by 'live leadership'—constant visits to
each hill position in turn, particularly where the enemy was
attacking, and he attacked several times a day, sometimes in
one sector and sometimes in another.

That same day a staff car drove up from the west and out
of it stepped General A. I. Eremenko. We embraced. It was
the first time we had seen each other since my release. I
thanked him for his courageous and kindly attitude towards
my wife after my arrest, and then told him about the situation at Yartsevo. Andrei Ivanovich saw the hopelessness of
our position but said: 'You must hold on whatever happens;
there are still other units of ours further to the west,' and
went off again in that direction.

The third day was exceptionally difficult as the enemy
attacked more and more persistently. Going from one hard-
pressed sector to another, I saw a soldier coming down from
a hillock bent under the weight of another man. He laid the
severely wounded man on the ground, and sat down near
him to rest. When I went up to them the wounded man was
clenching his teeth; his eyes were closed and his cheeks wet
with tears. When he heard us talking he opened his big grey
eyes and said as though justifying himself: 'I am not crying
from pain. I am crying because I promised myself not to die
until I had killed five Fascists, and now I have to die this

minute.' The medical orderly who had carried him down, said quickly, afraid of being too late: 'Five! You killed fifty, more like, with that machine-gun. I saw them falling under your bursts.' I don't know whether the orderly was telling the truth or just calming the dying man, but the latter then closed his grey eyes peacefully, and no more tears came from them.

And with such men in our army we were retreating!

On the fourth day, July 22nd, a full-strength division reached us and General Rokossovskii followed. That day, as I was inspecting our defences, I was hit at a range of about fifty yards by a German machine-gun crew who had slipped through our thin line under cover of night. When I had reported the situation to Rokossovskii, I was sent to hospital in Vyazma. There I discovered that our 25th Rifle Corps had been surrounded; various divisions and groups had escaped, but the corps commander and his staff had been taken prisoner. I was very shaken by this news.

Next morning I was flown to Moscow. I had a flesh wound just below the knee. The bone being undamaged, the wound healed quickly. Thirteen days later I was discharged from hospital.

I felt ashamed of walking around the streets of Moscow as long as there was no good news from the front. It seemed to me that everyone was looking at me, wanting to know why I was messing about in the rear when everything was going so badly at the front. I wanted to get back there quickly but no matter how hard I tried I could get no appointment. Corps Headquarters were being dismantled at this time. It was a month before I got an appointment, deep in the rear, to new duties in the area of Omsk. I managed to telephone my wife. When she heard that I was going to Omsk she was very happy and we decided that she should join me, so that we could spend some time together there while I was shaping up the troops.

Next day I went to visit Wilhelm Pieck at his hotel. He had heard about my arrest and greeted me with outstretched arms. Naturally we talked about the situation at the front and about Germany; we both firmly believed in the coming victory over Hitlerism and exchanged ideas about how victory would in fact be achieved. He recalled our meeting in 1936 when, raising a glass of wine, he had said: 'To our meeting in free Berlin!' 'Despite our great losses,' said Comrade Pieck, 'I believe that Fascism will be overcome and that we will indeed meet in a free Berlin.' After talking to me, Wilhelm Pieck telephoned Mekhlis and said to him: 'I've got Gorbatov here. He is back from the front to recover from a wound and has come to see me. He has seen a lot and can probably tell you more than he could tell me. Perhaps you could spare the time to see him.'

The following day, at one in the morning, there was a knock on my door. When I opened it an N.K.V.D. officer walked in, just as on the night of my arrest in 1938. He told me that Mekhlis had sent for me and that he was to take me to him. It is hard to describe my feelings as I was driven along the empty streets of Moscow that night. As soon as he saw me Mekhlis asked unpleasantly: 'Why are you behaving so deviously? Why didn't you come straight to me?' Without giving me a chance to reply Shchadenko, who was also present, added: 'It seems he didn't learn much in Kolyma.'

For a moment I was confused by such an unexpected greeting. Then, under questioning, I told them of my long acquaintanceship with Wilhelm Pieck, of what we had talked about and of my appointment to Omsk. There was in the way Mekhlis and Shchadenko talked to me a threatening undertone throughout, and when Mekhlis cancelled my posting to Omsk and ordered me to put my movement order on the table there was complete confusion in my mind.

My first sane thought was to telephone my wife. When I finally did get through I learned that she had already left on her long, tiring and now pointless journey to Omsk.

Luckily for me, Timoshenko was at that time commanding the southern sector. He had sent the head of his personnel department to select commanders from those in reserve. I was put first on the list of those travelling to the south.

On October 1st, 1941, in Kharkov, Colonel Portyannikov, the head of the personnel department, introduced the new officers to Commander-in-Chief of the South-Western Sector S. K. Timoshenko, and to N. S. Khrushchev, the Military Council member.

'I know Gorbatov well,' said the commander-in-chief and, turning to Khrushchev, added: 'He has recently been rehabilitated after returning from Kolyma. He has been wounded already. This one will fight.' Then, to me: 'Well, how's your wound? What shall we start with—cavalry or rifle troops?'

'My wound's doing fine,' I replied, 'and I'd like to start with a rifle division. I have been longing for a job of my own.'

'There's no difficulty about that sort of request,' said Timoshenko.

I was appointed there and then to command the 226th Rifle Division which was stationed twelve miles from Kharkov. As I was leaving Khrushchev said to me: 'Put all your strength and ability into instilling in your subordinates loyalty to their country and the Party, and confidence in our victory. And we shall have that victory, of course we shall have it—you know that yourself.'

I went back to the work which I had been doing nine

years earlier. Then, it had been a cavalry division in peace-time; now it was war and a rifle division. But that did not matter—my old experience stood me in good stead. And how I longed for real work! I found out from Colonel Portyannikov what jobs for senior officers were vacant in the division, then I went straight to the collecting point for front-line reserve officers, picked a group, my chief of staff, a young major named Boiko, among them, and with the officers I had chosen set off to join the division at the village of Olshany.

I spent the first few days getting to know the troops, dis-covering the mood of the soldiers and the officers and acquainting myself with the record of the division. After two days I called together the party activists, and held another meeting of senior officers, both to deal with the same questions: what we had to do to bring the division up to strength, and how to bring it into good fighting condition. What I had to say was supplemented by the head of the political department, Urev. Because of our continuing failures at the front we took account of the difficult frame of mind both of those who had been in the division for some time, and also of those who had just joined it. We were glad to find that among the new arrivals were veterans of the Civil War as well as old and young members of the Party and the Komsomol. These we considered a cement capable of binding together all the elements in the division.

Much later, in November, 1941, after our first encounter with the enemy and the fall of Kharkov, we analysed our losses during the retreat. Most of them had to be put down as missing, far more than were wounded or killed. The latter, for the most part, were officers, all of them Party and Komsomol members. We had made Party political work serve our main task, that of improving the division's tenacity in defence. But this did not satisfy us. We knew very well that even the most stubborn defence could not beat an army, and that while on the defensive we had to begin training our troops for attack. This meant that training and Party political work had to be backed up by active operations.

We discovered that the enemy had become over-confident after the successes of his summer advance and had moved for the winter into villages and clusters of houses between which lay large, unoccupied gaps. We decided to break through into the enemy's rear and destroy his garrisons. We thought that it could only be by killing Germans, or taking them prisoner, or at least getting some plunder, that our soldiers would come to believe in their own strength.

Our first raid was carried out on the village of Ogurtsovo in the German front line. We did not manage to take any prisoners but left ten enemy dead in the village. We captured a mortar, some rifles, grenades, cartridges, horses and carts, food, the papers of the dead, uniforms, bedding, underwear, and other things. We lost one man killed. From this single small raid we became convinced that our work had not gone for nothing and that we could attack the enemy's rear on a much larger scale.

These operations had three main purposes: to show the enemy that we were able to strike him hard; to convince our men of their own capabilities; and to establish to our own satisfaction that our battalions were ready for battle.

The village of Korovino was the target of our second operation. There was a battery of 4-inch guns in this village which had been causing us a great deal of trouble by systematically bombarding our line and the village of Shebekino. It was necessary for the purposes of the operation to cover the roads leading to Korovino. To make sure of this we decided to take one battalion from each regiment and a reconnaissance company from the division, and to attach a sapper officer and eight men with explosives to them. Because of its importance for us I decided to command this operation myself.

The night of November 20th was warm. There was low cloud. Unobserved by the enemy we crossed the Northern Donets and went through the woods. We made our last halt in a cutting leading up from the river. Here we closed up the column, went over the orders which we had previously arranged, and checked over the agreed signals, the rendez-vous and the line of retreat. When we moved off again to cover the last five hundred yards the vanguard reported to me: 'We saw two men coming towards us, heard a shout in German and then running footsteps. They have gone back to the village.' It was clear that these two had spotted us and gone back to warn their comrades.

We had to press on quickly now that the enemy had had a few moments to get himself ready. We quickened our pace in order to begin the attack fifteen minutes earlier than sche-duled. All units attacked the village simultaneously and with determination, but the element of surprise had been lost, and by 0730 hours the enemy was still holding the houses in whose gardens the battery was sited. Part of the battalion of the 989th Rifle Regiment faltered and began to go back into the forest, but we were able to stop them. The action dragged on. The enemy fought doggedly, but we were resolved not to leave things half-finished and by 0830 hours we had com-pletely overrun the village and destroyed the garrison. Only some twenty Germans managed to run away and many of these were shot by our covering party, which also fired on the enemy reinforcements trying to break through to Korovino.

In this action the enemy lost at least three times as many men as we did, and we destroyed a 4-inch gun battery, eight motor vehicles, some ammunition and carts, took sixteen prisoners, and carried away iron rations, cameras, food and a great many other things. Moreover, every one of our soldiers who took part—more than a thousand men—managed to win some personal trophies.

We had carried out our task. I was delighted to notice the good discipline, not only on the march but in action. Almost none of our men had gone missing. Among the faults we reckoned a lack of quick, bold action by some men and officers, and inadequate use of cover under artillery fire; and some sub-units still reacted badly to shouts of 'They're out-flanking us,' and 'They're surrounding us.'

To conclude my memories of 1941 let me recount one small but characteristic episode. An instructor from the army political department arrived at divisional headquarters one day. He called on me with the divisional commissar and reported that he had come to investigate the immoral conduct of Lieutenant-Colonel X, commander of the nth Rifle Regiment, 'about whom there has been a signal to the political department.' When I enquired what particular form this officer's 'immoral' conduct had taken, the instructor replied: 'He is living with a doctor.' Visiting X I had met in his quarters an extremely pleasant woman doctor of about 40. I knew that they came from the same town and had friends in common. I told the instructor this and added: 'Have you really got nothing better to do? Have you not got anything more important than this to occupy you in these hard times?' He was silent. I asked him who had sent him, but got no clear reply. I felt that I must make it absolutely clear where I stood on this point. 'Firstly, I will not allow this kind of thing to be raised as an issue in this division. It seems to me that to bring to light intimate personal matters would merely hurt and offend the people involved and adversely affect their fighting potential. And secondly, if I had gone into X's room or his dug-out and found him and the doctor in bed together I would have quietly shut the door and never said a word about it, either to them or to anybody else. It would have been a different matter if she had complained that he was pestering her, or was behaving badly, but this was clearly not happening.' The instructor from the political department then left.

On December 22nd, 1941, I was promoted to the rank of Major-General. The army commander handed me a fur cap with the general's insignia and said: 'I am presenting you with this as a sign of the complete trust reposed in you by our Party and Government, and I congratulate you on reaching your first—though, I am convinced, not your last—general officer's rank.' I thanked him as the representative of the Party and Government for the trust which they had reposed in me, and thanked him personally for his good wishes. Many members of our division were decorated with orders and medals for our three raids. I was among them and was awarded the Order of the Red Banner.

In November, 1941, Rostov-on-Don was freed from the enemy in the south; in the north Tikhvin was also liberated, and in December we learned of the German collapse near Moscow. These first but great successes of the Soviet Army were the best proof that the future was ours. Nevertheless the winter campaign was an extremely difficult one. At that time the Germans were still fighting bitterly to the last man; they seldom surrendered, and then only when there was no other way out. They often fought on when they were completely surrounded, and went on fighting until reinforcements reached them, often from a long way away.

In an order dated January 10th, 1942, the Supreme Command required that we should not give the Germans any breathing space but should, using forces with a concentration of manpower three to four times greater than that of the enemy, break down his positions in depth, covering our advance with artillery fire, and that not only with opening barrages but with powerful artillery support throughout the offensive operations.

The Supreme Command's order was full of great good sense and would have led to success if everything it said had been well carried out. But we continued to receive orders which bore little relation to the G.H.Q. requirements and so our successes were few. It is difficult to understand why such orders should have come even from our own army commander, of whom I thought highly.

In this situation it was natural enough that divisional commanders should choose individual objectives for themselves and determine the make-up of detachments and the timing of operations to safeguard the element of surprise in the light of the local situation and means of approach. In such cases the enemy usually suffered losses two, three and even four times greater than our own. It was a different matter when somebody sitting miles away wrote out orders for you to seize, on January 17th, Maslova Pristan, on January 19th, Bezlyudofovka, on January 24th, Arkhangelskoe, and so on, with precise instructions as to the hour of the attack and the size of the detachment—instructions which, on top of everything else, corresponded neither to your task nor to your capabilities. In these cases the result was almost always the same: we had no success and suffered losses two or three times greater than the enemy's.

What was most difficult of all to understand were the

insistent orders to repeat the attack, despite failure, from exactly the same point of departure, in exactly the same direction, several days on the run—without taking into account that the enemy would already have strengthened this sector of his position.

Many, many times on such occasions my heart wept blood. Yet this was a stage in the war when many of our officers learned how not to fight and consequently how they should fight. The slowness with which this knowledge was absorbed—no matter how obvious were the bloody examples —was the result of those pre-war conditions in which the mental habits of the officers had been formed.

In March our 226th Rifle Division was transferred to the 38th Army. On March 4th we formed up six miles east of Verkhnii Saltov, and on March 5th received our first orders: on the night of the 6th we were to relieve units of the 300th Rifle Division, and on the 7th to go into the attack.

On the 6th, after we had completed the relief, my divisional chief of staff and I, the regimental and battalion commanders and those in charge of other detachments of troops, carried out a reconnaissance. When we had got to know the locality we worked out a concerted plan of action.

On the day of the attack there was an exceptionally heavy blizzard for that part of the country. Visibility was down to twenty yards. The platoon commanders could not see their men, the companies and battalions could not be controlled and so our attack, and that of our neighbours, was unsuccessful. At 1800 hours I reported failure to the army commander.

'Whom do you serve?' he asked.

'I serve the Soviet people and our Party, Comrade General,' I replied, and asked his permission to say what I thought of the situation. He agreed and I continued: 'The

village of Verkhnii Saltov which we were to take stretches
for more than a mile along a single street on the western bank
of the river. In front of it is a broad, open valley. Behind the
village there is a height from which the enemy dominates the
area lying before him for some two miles. I suggest that the
enemy observed the relief of the 300th Division. He brought
up reserves and strengthened his fighting units. There was no
surprise at the beginning of the attack and so there is even
less chance of success now. Even if we do manage to take
Verkhnii Saltov it will be at far too high a price.'

'Come to the point! What are you suggesting?' broke in
the army commander, '—that we cancel the advance by
your divisions?'

'No, that's not what I want,' I replied. 'The enemy is in a
very favourable position, with riflemen and machine-gunners
in every one of the hundred and fifty huts stretching over
about a mile and a half of the front. We would be forced to
expose ourselves to his fire. So a frontal attack in this sector is
not the best idea. I doubt also whether my colleagues have
managed to take Rubezhnoe and Staryi Saltov.'

'You have a pretty poor opinion of your colleagues,'
observed the army commander. 'You'd do better to improve
your own performance.'

I went on to propose that for a start the two divisions, my
colleague's to the right and my own, should combine to take
the village of Rubezhnoe. From there my colleague would
attack in the direction marked out for him in the first place,
while we attacked to the south towards the flank and rear of
the enemy in Verkhnii Saltov. This way we would be sure of
taking Rubezhnoe, and by outflanking Verkhnii Saltov
would come under fire not from a hundred and fifty huts but
only from the two huts at the end, thereby reducing our
losses and proportionately increasing our chances of success.

Once we had taken Verkhnii Saltov we could help the other division to our left by continuing the attack towards Staryi Saltov. On these grounds I asked permission to detach a large part of my forces to take part in the attack on the village of Rubezhnoe. After a short pause I got: 'I don't object. Arrange it with Ter-Gasparian, only don't hold up the execution of my general order.'

As I had expected the commander of the 277th Rifle Division and I had no difficulty in agreeing on joint action against Rubezhnoe. On March 8th we were busy regrouping and did not attack. On the 9th we managed to take fifteen huts in Rubezhnoe, and by midday on the 10th, with the help of two tanks, we had got control of half the village. While we were fighting near the church and I was about a hundred yards from it I was handed two documents bearing the seal of the Military Council of the Army. In rude and insulting terms they accused the divisional command of shameful actions bordering on crime. I read these documents, returned them to the despatch rider who had brought them and ordered him to go back.

Towards 1700 hours my colleague and I had cleared Rubezhnoe of the enemy, and I ordered the start of the attack on Verkhnii Saltov. On the 11th we liberated Verkhnii Saltov and Petrovskoye, and on the 12th took the big market village of Staryi Saltov and the even bigger village of Molodovoye. In three days' fighting we had captured 42 guns, 51 mortars, 71 machine-guns, 55 stens, 400 rifles, 82 horses, 16 field kitchens, 72 carts, 41 dumps of ammunition, food and clothing and much other booty. On March 13th we took the villages of Fedoroveka, Oktyabrskoye, Peschanoye and Dragunovka on our right flank and, by overlapping on our right flank, gave our comrades on that side some very real help. That day the 989th Rifle Division, badly depleted, covered the open right flank of the other regiments which had moved a long way forward, and held the villages we had taken.

At midday the enemy launched a counter-attack from the village of Nepokrytoye on Peschanoye. This attack was repulsed after hard fighting. Of the Germans who attacked Peschanoye fifty-six were taken prisoner. It should be remembered that, at that time, so well were the opposing sides matched that an advance of a single half-mile was regarded as an achievement, while a single prisoner taken by a patrol while we were on the defensive earned a medal.

Before evening the enemy, as if trying to avenge the prisoners he had lost, launched another counter-attack, this time with tanks accompanied by an intensive bombardment from twenty-six aircraft. We had to leave Peschanoye. Our consciences were clear: we had done everything that had been asked of us and dealt the enemy a bitter blow. However, this did not put an end to the accusations which were showered on the division.

I should not pass on without saying that the successes we had achieved in the six days of the operation were entirely due to the heroism shown by all the men, and the initiative and determination of the officers. All the orders from army headquarters arrived late. For example, according to one order we were supposed to begin an advance on Chervona Roganna at 1000 hours on March 15th. We had already taken it on the 14th. The orders bore little relation to what was going on.

On March 22nd we received another order—it was distributed throughout the army—in which we were accused of retreating and deserting the village of Peschanoye after an enemy attack by two companies supported by tanks. This information, the order said, had been gleaned from enemy prisoners under interrogation.

I called the army commander to the telephone and asked him where he had got such absurd information from. 'If you read my orders carefully, you will see that they state where we got it from,' was the supercilious answer I received.

'We reported to you that the first counter-attack against Peschanoye was repulsed at midday on March 14th, not by units of the 226th Rifle Division, but one platoon of the 989th Rifle Regiment, and that we took prisoners. It was only as a result of the second enemy counter-attack with superior forces of infantry and tanks, and under severe bombardment from the air, that we left the village. Why do you prefer to believe a German prisoner rather than me? Why didn't you ask the prisoner this simple question: "If our men left the village as soon as they saw the Germans, then who took you and the other fifty-five prisoners?" I consider your order an outright invention and a slander against the 226th Division.'

That evening I telephoned Marshal Timoshenko and asked him to see me together with the army commander so that we could clear the matter up in his presence. A few days later I set off to G.H.Q. taking with me seven orders published by Army H.Q. over the last ten days, in which officers and divisional commanders were reprimanded. I decided to tell the Military Council of the Front everything in its proper sequence, beginning with the pointless and constant attacks on the same objectives for as long as ten or fifteen days at a time, regardless of the fact that we were suffering heavy losses.

When I went in to see Marshal Timoshenko, N. S. Khrushchev, the Military Council member, Chief of Staff I. Kh. Bagramian and the G.O.C. 38th Army were already there. After I had introduced myself, Timoshenko said: 'Now, tell us, what's the trouble?'

I had been brought to white heat by the insults which had been heaped upon me. I pointed my finger at the army commander and shouted: 'Do you call that man an army commander!'

Khrushchev came up to me and putting his hand on my shoulder said reproachfully: 'Comrade Gorbatov, surely that isn't the right way to talk about an army commander, particularly in wartime?'

'I have no patience left. I have said what I think. In five days our division took more than a hundred prisoners, besides dozens of guns and mortars, and all because we acted on our own initiative and in spite of the orders of the army commander. All that the leadership provided by the army commander amounts to is a totally unpardonable attitude towards the men under him. I am sick and tired of listening to his everlasting abuse. How can the army commander fail to understand that his conduct, far from encouraging his subordinates, only succeeds in destroying their faith in their own ability? I was treated to insults like this from the interrogators in Lefortovo Prison, and I don't want to hear any more of them. We are all serving and will go on serving our country and our Party honestly, but undeserved abuse from any man can only have a bad effect. I ask you to shield us from it.'

The commander-in-chief said, turning to the army commander: 'I warned you that rudeness was not permissible but you have taken no notice of my remarks. You must put a stop to it.' To me he said: 'You shouldn't get so excited, Comrade Gorbatov. We will sort this out.' He asked me about the state of the division and, when he had made sure that the Military Council member had no questions

for me, gave me permission to return to my headquarters.

Throughout all this the army commander had not said a
single word. When I left he stayed with the commander-in-
chief.

When I got back to the division I thought over everything
that I had said and heard. I cursed myself for having got so
angry. There was no need to answer rudeness with rudeness.
What I should have done was to have told everything calmly
and in the right order. 'But no,' I said to myself, 'it couldn't
have been any other way. Let the Military Council bring
him to order.'

After my visit to the Military Council the number of
insulting orders became noticeably less. But the army
commander completely ignored me and communicated
with me only through his chief of staff, General Ivanov. For
me it was a pleasure to have dealings with Ivanov; I
respected him for his coolness and his knowledge of affairs.

On June 22nd I was appointed Inspector of Cavalry to
the Headquarters of the South-Western Sector. I cannot say
that I was pleased with this appointment. I had served
twenty-eight years in the cavalry and I liked this arm better
than any other. But with the appearance of air forces and
tank brigades, starting in 1935, I began to have serious
doubts about the role which cavalry would play in any
future war, particularly in the western theatre. It was for
this very reason that just before the beginning of the war I
had made plain my desire to serve in general troop formations. The first year of the war confirmed my opinion.
Besides, the duties of an inspector, which consisted in large
measure of purely office work, were contrary to my nature—
more than anything else I loathed scribbling reports. I

suffered these duties for three months, trying to find something in them, something worth doing, something I could do with pleasure.

In August our Inspecting Commission was in Stalingrad. To me, who throughout the last ten months had never been out of gunshot range of the enemy, the town was striking in its everyday, almost peacetime aspect. It was strange to see so many people wearing civilian clothes, enjoying themselves in the warm evenings on the banks of the Volga. The inhabitants seemed surprised at the arrival of front headquarters in their town. This invasion soon overlaid the earlier picture of a town deep in the rear with the stamp of a front-line base. The nearer the front approached and the more soldiers appeared, the more pressing and feverish became the life of the town. Then the evacuation began. The second echelon of front headquarters transferred to the eastern bank.

I found it quite intolerable to be on the far side of the Volga. Leaving a colonel to look after my duties, I drove out to see Eremenko, who had been appointed commander of the front.

His command point was set up in one of the ravines. N. S. Khrushchev, the Military Council member, and A. N. Vasilevskii were with Eremenko when I arrived. I could see from their faces that I had not come at the best possible time. Nevertheless I introduced myself and we exchanged greetings.

'It's a long time since we met, Comrade Gorbatov,' said Eremenko. 'What have you got to say for yourself?'

'I can't stand being stuck over on the eastern bank. Please give me some kind of operational work to do. The inactivity of an inspector's life is choking me and my colonel could perfectly well cope.'

It seemed to me that Khrushchev made some sort of sign in reply to Eremenko's questioning look.

'Come back in about an hour,' Eremenko said.

I returned exactly an hour later. The commander said: 'Well, there it is. This is the situation: the enemy has forced a crossing of the Don, and is bearing down on the Volga—towards the southern edge of Stalingrad, I imagine. Our corps of three rifle divisions is coming down from the north.' He indicated a road on the map. 'You must go to meet them and dispose them for the defence of the south-western sector of the town.' He sketched out the line of defence on my map. When he was certain that I had understood my task, he said: 'Well, good luck then, and hurry.'

I was delighted to have got a job to do, albeit a temporary one. When I had gone as far as the village of Gorodishche I met one division, found its commander and told him what I wanted him to do. Further on, beyond Gorodishche, I came up with the second division and gave its commander his orders. But as I drove on to meet the third division, I suddenly saw tanks moving across open country in two columns. They were followed by infantry in motor vehicles and a large number of aircraft were circling overhead. I had no doubt that this was the enemy and that he was making not for the southern but for the northern edge of the town. What was I to do?

I decided, first, not to go on towards the third division (indeed, I could not have done so, as I would have been cut off from Stalingrad); secondly, to change my orders to the divisions which I had met already; but before anything else, to make for the anti-aircraft batteries, which were sited quite near the road and were firing at the enemy aircraft, so as to change their orders as well. I went up to the nearest battery. Fortunately I found an anti-aircraft colonel on the gun-site and, pointing out the enemy tank and infantry columns to him, I ordered all anti-aircraft guns in the area to fire at ground targets rather than aircraft. The colonel, while I was still there, ordered the troop to lower their guns and begin firing on the tanks. He promised to pass on these orders to the other troops. Under the hail of anti-aircraft shells the enemy columns broke formation. Hoping that the gunfire would put the third division on its guard and that the enemy would not catch it unawares, I caught up with the first two divisions, explained the change in the situation to their commanding officers and indicated the new defence lines for the north-western outskirts of the town.

It all turned out very well. The divisions, instead of having to go some nine miles further, went into position almost where they stood, individual units moving two to three miles forward to meet the enemy. I advised the divisional commanders to get their artillery sited immediately, to push out observers and to open artillery fire even before the defence areas had been manned by the rifle units. I told them how to communicate with the front headquarters command post and went back myself to report to the front commander.

Trying to restrain my excitement I entered the building. 'Well, did you meet them?' he asked. I reported what I had seen, what I had done and where the command posts of the two divisions had been set up. It was clear that I was the first to report how close the enemy was and that he was going not to the south but to the northern edge of Stalingrad. The commander thanked me and immediately sent me to the tractor factory where tanks were being repaired, to order the despatch of all tanks that were operational to support the two rifle divisions. He also ordered me to go out to the Military Academy, in the northern part of the town, and get it ready for action as a fighting unit. It was late at night when I got back, tired but pleased with my day's work.

The following day the enemy reached the Volga north of Stalingrad near the village of Rynok. From that day on I began to carry out many varied operational duties.

At this time the Don Front was being organised, with K. K. Rokossovskii as its commander and A. S. Zheltov as the Military Council member. As there were no cavalry on the Stalingrad Front I was appointed Inspector of Cavalry for the Don Front.

As I left the town it was already one sheet of flame and no attempt was being made to put out the fires anywhere. It would have been impossible, anyway. I had to send my staff car back to headquarters from the harbour, and my driver and I crossed to the eastern bank of the Volga at Krasnaya Sloboda, on the ferry, and made our way from there along the eastern bank via Kamyshin towards the headquarters of the Don Front.

A day later I was with Rokossovskii and was soon posted to a mixed cavalry corps which was charged with a most important task—the defence of a bridgehead on the western bank of the Don.

In these troubled times I often ruminated on how it could have happened that we had been forced back to the Volga: could this be explained simply by the unexpectedness of the enemy's onslaught? It seemed to me that there was more to it than that and I increasingly inclined to the opinion that one of the basic reasons for our failures at the front was the lack of properly qualified officers: so many of our most experienced divisional commanders were still cooped up in Kolyma, while at the front the command of units and larger formations had to be entrusted to people who, although honest and loyal and willing to die for their country, did not know how to fight. When units suffered losses these were made up with people who had long been out of the army. Some of them had forgotten their military training; others reached the units without even acquainting themselves with the new weapons and equipment. They had not even been taught the absolute essentials. All this was aggravated by the incompetent choice of men, for which Sasha Rumyantsev was responsible. I saw how he selected his officers and how he talked to people. He was incapable of judging the operational qualities of officers, and was interested only in their security records. To jump ahead a little, when I was in Moscow after the fighting on the Volga, I found that Rumyantsev had already been removed from the post of Deputy for Personnel to the Supreme Commander. I was also pleased to discover that Shchadenko was no longer responsible for military training.

In April, 1943, I became a lieutenant-general, and in June was appointed to command the 3rd Army which was defending the Mtsensk area on the river Zusha. The first thing I did was to visit the headquarters of the Bryansk Front in order to introduce myself to the front commander, Mark Mikhailovich Popov, and to L. Z. Mekhlis, the Military Council member.

The front commander received me extremely well, asked me to tell him briefly about my service career and suggested that I should stay the night so that his deputy, General Fedyuninskii, could take me to the 3rd Army in the morning. When I told him I wanted to meet the Military Council member he added: 'Come back in an hour and have dinner with me.'

I was somewhat on my guard as I went to see Mekhlis, remembering my conversation with him and Shchadenko in

September, 1941, in Moscow. As I introduced myself to him I met a sharp, questioning look. But this was not the old Mekhlis—it was obvious that his severe failure at Kerch had left its mark.

'So you have been posted here?' said Mekhlis.

'Yes, to your front,' I replied.

'All right—get to know your army. Next time we meet you can give me a report on it. Then we'll talk.' And that was all.

On closer acquaintance over dinner, I found to my great delight that the front commander was a young but thoroughly well-informed general, and a resourceful and cheerful man. Of the army which I was to take over he said: 'It's dug itself into the ground. It's gone stale in defence. It has carried out a number of unsuccessful offensive operations, but all that is in the past.' He stressed that. 'I'll say nothing about the officers now so as not to prejudice you. Only one thing— there are no hopeless cases among them. What we all need is work, work and more work—generals as much as men.'

Early next morning Fedyuninskii and I went out to the 3rd Army Headquarters in the village of Yerzhino. Fedyuninskii introduced me as the new commander to the senior officers and to the generals. I was to take part in many glorious and hard battles with the 3rd Army, of which I will only be able to mention a few here.

On July 18th, 1943, we were advancing on Orel. I was with the 380th Division on the left flank when I heard that the sector, which was wide enough already, had been further increased by six miles at the expense of our neighbour on the left. If previously the task of liberating Orel had been the job of the 63rd Army with some help from us, it now lay entirely with us. Our neighbour in the line was pulling out; we had to decide quickly how to fill his space and how to group our forces for the conquest of Orel. The opinion was put forward at a meeting which I called that we should build up a powerful force on our left flank. It was by no means clear, however, where the men and equipment were going to come from; our army's sector was now about forty miles wide, and one and a half of our divisions were still back on the river Zusha on a front twenty-five miles wide. I pointed out that the town of Orel is divided into two equal parts—the eastern and the western—by the River Oka, and that the western part of the town is in its turn divided into north and south by the River Orlik. If we were to set up a force to attack the town from the east, and succeed, while the enemy retained the western half, we would be forced to subject the latter to artillery fire and bombing. The enemy would do the same, and between us we would completely destroy the eastern half of the town. If we were to occupy the southern part of the western half of the town, a similar situation would arise: we and the enemy between us would again be driven to destroy the town. Was it therefore, in fact, the best idea to attack the town from the east? Should we not try to find another answer?

After much debate and discussion we decided to take Orel by outflanking it from the north and north-west. We would set up a task force on our right flank, and force the Oka at a point some fifteen to twenty miles north of the town. By attacking from the north-west we would threaten the enemy with encirclement if he tried to hold the River Zusha and the town of Mtsensk. By striking along the western bank of the Oka and outflanking Orel we would again be in a position to envelop the enemy if he thought of defending the town. What is more, we would in this way avoid street fighting, the destruction of the town and unnecessary losses. We decided not to strengthen our left flank. On the contrary, we would stretch the 41st Corps over a further six miles and only have one division of this corps attacking from the east, while the remaining two would cross the Oka north of Orel.

This decision was fully justified in practice. While we turned the main body of the army to the north-west, Colonel Chervonii, the energetic and far-sighted commander of the 342nd Rifle Division, left one regiment to hold a twenty-mile front on the bank of the Zusha, concentrated the rest of the division opposite Mtsensk, and carefully watched the enemy. As soon as the latter began to withdraw Chervonii's division forced the Zusha along the whole of his front and set off in pursuit. It is true that, after crossing the river, Chervonii spent rather too long in the comfort of the well built dug-outs which the Germans had left behind and lagged behind his regiments—I had to go off in my staff car and drop him where he should have been—but he never found occasion to use my car again!

On reaching the rivers Oka and Optukha we established a number of bridgeheads on the Oka, and strengthened and broadened them.

I visited the 308th Division on the evening of August 2nd, to rebuke its commander, General Gortev, usually a most energetic man, because he had not done enough to exploit the gains of neighbouring divisions. The next morning my observation post was five hundred yards from the enemy on the northern bank of the Nepolod. I could see Orel through my glasses and I heard a series of dull explosions in the town. Clouds of black smoke were rising over it—the Germans were blowing up stores and buildings.

About this time a report arrived from General Gortev that his units had occupied Krolchatnik. This was extremely important—Krolchatnik was the enemy's main support point on the way to the town. But when I turned my glasses in that direction I could see that Krolchatnik was still in

enemy hands. I was sure that by then the divisional commander would already have transferred his command post
and discovered for himself the error in the report. Gortev
was an independent-minded, honest and determined officer.
I could well imagine how much he had taken to heart my
remarks of the previous day, and now his subordinates had
misled him over Krolchatnik. I felt extremely sorry for him.
I was afraid that he might go wild and try to force progress
out of them, and so decided to go out and try to cheer him up.
His observation post was in an open field between the railway
and the road, about a mile from Krolchatnik. 'Yes,' I thought,
'he is probably itching to go in himself!'

The site for the observation post had been very badly
chosen: one could see frequent shell bursts over it. Leaving
my car in a clump of trees by the railway, I walked across a
field of rye. The rye was very short but we repeatedly had to
lie down in it to wait for shell bursts. My appearance at the
observation post surprised Gortev. He was embarrassed and
started talking too fast.

'What are you doing here, Comrade Commander? You'd
better come straight down into my dug-out—the enemy has
got our range down to the zero mark.'

I jumped down into the narrow slit. We were bunched up
against each other. Gortev was apparently expecting another
rebuke, so I said: 'Things are going well today. I'm sure you
will soon have Krolchatnik.'

He sighed with relief, and cheered up. I was glad, because
I valued his humility, almost his shyness, combined as it was
with the very best qualities of an officer.

At this moment the enemy's guns opened up again. 'Get
down lower, that's for us,' yelled Gortev.

The trench was shallow and although we were sitting down
our heads still stuck out above ground. A shell burst some

ten or fifteen paces in front of us. I thought I had been hit on
the head but it was only mild shock. Gortev got up and said:
'Comrade Commander, I think I am killed,' and his head
dropped on to my shoulder.

He had been killed. He left his blood on my uniform jacket
and cap for me to remember him by. I kept this jacket and
cap to the very end of the war. The Military Council of the
Army expressed its deepest sympathy with the 308th Rifle
Division on the loss of their commanding officer, a first-class
general, a Communist and one of the most valiant defenders
of Stalingrad. Leontii Nikolaevich Gortev was posthumously
awarded the title of Hero of the Soviet Union.

On the same day the Military Council issued a proclamation to all soldiers and officers in our army; 'Soldiers and
officers! Under your very eyes Hitler's bandits are destroying
Orel. You are between four and six miles from the town.
Two or three hours of rapid advance will not merely save you
unnecessary casualties, it will prevent the enemy from wreck-
ing for good our own town. Forward to its immediate liberation!' This appeal was brought to the notice of every officer
and soldier.

On August 4th Kustov's division and the 17th Tank
Brigade commanded by Colonel Shulgin broke into the
eastern part of the town; units of the 308th Division, after
crossing the Oka near Shchekotikhin, came in from the
north, while the task force, having crossed the Nekolod,
enveloped the town from the north-west along the western
bank of the Oka. From the south units of the 5th and 169th
Rifle Divisions entered the town. By 1745 hours Orel was
completely clear of Germans. The population of the town
gave a triumphant welcome to its liberators. While delayed-
action mines were still going off in the town I went to visit the
station area and went round the ruined barracks in which I

had served from 1912 to the beginning of the First World War. I also visited the gully where our rifle range had been. Thanks to the October Revolution it had fallen to the lot of a former private soldier to command the army which had liberated this town, where thirty years ago he had served as a simple trooper.

The Member of the Military Council for the Front, Mekhlis, was apparently one of those people who have too long a memory and have great difficulty in changing their opinion about people. I did not doubt that he well remembered his rudeness to me in his office in Moscow after my meeting with Wilhelm Pieck, and had not forgotten taking my movement order from me. After that interview I had not slept for several nights, expecting the worst, and had been extremely relieved when Timoshenko chose me to serve with him in the south.

Right up to the liberation of Orel, Mekhlis always took the opportunity, whenever we met, of asking me certain questions and trying to drive me into a corner. I made my answers simple, and probably often not on the lines he might have wished. However it was noticeable that, albeit with difficulty on his part, our relationship was improving.

When we had taken Orel, he suddenly said to me: 'I have been watching you for a long time and I must say that I like you both as an army commander and as a Communist. I have been following every step you have made since you left Moscow but I never quite believed the good I heard of you. Now I see that I was wrong.'

I thanked him for his frankness and did not conceal the fact that I had not liked him very much either and had spent many unpleasant hours worrying about it. I had also noticed how cautiously he had received me at the front. Fortunately, it was my habit to put the job in hand first.

After this conversation Mekhlis began to visit us more often. He would even stay to drink tea—a most unusual thing for him to do. He was an indefatigable, severe, mistrustful man, single-minded to the point of fanaticism, a man of extreme opinions and completely inflexible—which is why, for all his energy, he often did not get good results. It was characteristic of him that he would never let anyone else write messages for him; he wrote them all himself in his own very unusual handwriting.

I should have liked to write about every operation in which we took part. The conditions under which the 3rd Army was working, and the characters of the people who had come together in its command, and who soon came to share a common outlook, were such that no single operation was carried out as a carbon copy of another. Every time we tried to find the solution best fitted to the particular circumstances. I shall not attempt to assess our results from a broad theoretical point of view but it seems to me that the description and analysis of an individual operation has just as much value as the repetition of rules and methods put forward as if they were uniformly applicable to any similar situation. That is not the whole of it, however. Even when I held senior appointments my relations with my subordinates were never restricted to service formalities, and this in spite of the fact that I was a very exacting commander. It may be that the soldiers and junior officers felt in me a man who had been through a good deal in his life. At any rate, they treated me, for the most part, with a degree of openness, and something personal in their attitude, which was nevertheless entirely compatible with the respect due to seniors. Many faces and many names are imprinted in my memory. If I had the strength and the ability I would write about these 'inconspicuous heroes,' who combined greatness of heart with simplicity of action, flexibility with strength of mind. Here I can only refer to a few and, needless to say, I must also omit many very important episodes of the war. But these reminiscences of mine are not meant to be history, not even a history of the army which I commanded.

I shall not speak here of the battles on the Dnieper and the river Drut, or of the first days of the liberation of Soviet Belorussia, but I shall go straight on to those operations which crowned the part played by the 3rd Army in the Great Patriotic War against Fascism.

ELEVEN

The Advance on Berlin

After we had liberated Minsk on July 3rd, 1944, the enemy put up stubborn resistance only in those areas that most favoured defence, and around important objectives. After we had covered a hundred and twenty-five miles in ten days of heavy fighting we began to advance west at a rate of fifteen to twenty-five miles a day, detaching a reinforced regiment from each division to act as cover guard, and pursued the enemy along parallel lines.

Shortly afterwards our army was transferred from the 1st to the 2nd Belorussian Front, and we began to feel an acute shortage of all necessities. This was particularly serious because groups of the enemy far in our rear had not yet been liquidated.

We sent a report full of alarm to H.Q., 2nd Belorussian Front. At the same time we issued strict instructions for economy to corps and divisional commanders so as not to run out of any requisites, as we could hope for no improvement in supply during the next four days. They were to make greater use of all captured ammunition; disable captured trucks and staff cars; supply fuel only to vehicles carrying guns and mortars; jettison from transport all inessentials—cupboards, chairs, tables, and so on; and bring all victuals under strict control so that every ounce of rations for the men got into their stomachs and nowhere else.

Army headquarters warned the formation commanders

that in the areas we were about to reach the enemy might try to counter-attack at any time. Carelessness, therefore, either on the march, in camp at night or during rest, was not permissible. Incidentally, during the previous few days, when the enemy had offered only weak resistance and our troops had been moving forward quickly, discipline on the march had slackened; occasionally artillery mortars and even machine-guns had separated from the infantry, and some battalions had simply been advancing as a mob. There had been occasions when reconnaissance and cover detachments on the march and at local halts had not been sent out at all. The commanders tended to explain this away by the weariness of their men, and their hope that the enemy would not attack, particularly as there was army cover in front of them. Formations and units approached rivers and areas suitable for defence positions piecemeal, often giving no thought as to how they might capture them. Army headquarters reminded the commanders that all this could lead to painful results. The enemy was not beaten yet; rather he was thoroughly roused and we could expect every sort of wily reaction from him.

We were not wrong in warning our commanders to stay on their guard: on the river Servich the enemy offered very stubborn resistance. True enough, even here his defences were quickly broken down. The first to cross was the 120th Guards Division which went over at night against heavy opposition and drove the enemy into a general retreat at dawn. In this battle Divisional Commander Yan Yanovich Fogel was, as always, at the head of his men. He was severely wounded and died. This was a great loss. We had lost an old Bolshevik, a fine commander respected by all and a splendid comrade-in-arms. He was buried with suitable honours in the village of Dyatlovo. That was not the only loss we suffered among senior commanders. As we approached the western border of Belorussia we were saddened by a new loss. The commander of the 35th Rifle Corps, Viktor Grigorevich Zholudev, was killed. He was posthumously awarded the title of Hero of the Soviet Union.

Zholudev's death happened like this. After the liberation of the town of Volkovysk, the strongest enemy mass was opposite our right flank where General Zholudev's corps was situated and, as a result, held up. Early in the morning of July 28th I telephoned General Zholudev, told him where the divisions of the 40th and 41st Corps were located, and asked him how things were with him.

'Bad,' he replied sadly.

'The divisional and regimental commanders aren't falling behind the fighting units, are they?' I asked.

'It would appear not.'

'I will come and see you.'

When I arrived at corps headquarters I was told that General Zholudev had gone out to the 323rd Rifle Division. Making sure of the route I set out after him, first to the divisional command post and then on to the observation post, about half a mile further on. There I found hurried preparations under way to move the observation post elsewhere—by no means a bad idea, as from its existing site visibility was extremely restricted. The corps commander and the divisional commander were standing by their cars, ready to leave. I did not want to hold them up and merely asked whether they knew their way to the newly selected observation post, and whether communications had yet been established with it. They replied 'Yes' to both questions. The corps commander left his own car behind and drove ahead in the divisional commander's. I followed them.

There were no clearly defined roads—the area was broken

country. We drove first along a field road, and then along a forest track towards the west. Then the leading car bore south-west along a slightly better road. Then it turned north. It became clear to me that the divisional commander did not know his way to the new observation post. During a momentary stop I heard the corps commander rebuking him for this. I kept clear so as not to embarrass the divisional commander and mix him up completely, and went on following them.

When we came out on a good field track, open country lay on our right and the forest on our left. Along the track stood a row of three widely spaced houses and about a mile beyond them there rose the high hill towards which we were driving.

It seemed suspicious to me that there was no sign of men, vehicles or gun emplacements on the slope facing us. I told my driver to catch up with the leading car and sound his horn. When we got near them I shouted: 'Don't stop. Keep going, but drive slowly and listen carefully to me; you obviously do not know where you are going. I will count up to three. On the count of three, all of you jump from the car and make a dash for the back of the house!' Then to my own driver; 'As soon as we've jumped, make a quick turn and get back behind the hill.'

When we got to the last house Zholudev, Maslov, my orderly officer and I jumped from the cars and ran round behind the house. At that very moment three machine-guns and about a dozen rifles opened fire on us. The divisional commander's car was shot as full of holes as a sieve. My own car vanished at high speed behind clouds of dust like a smoke screen. Bullets flew along the road, pinging on the wrecked car and lodging in the walls of the house.

The enemy was two hundred yards from us in a well-concealed trench. It was clear that the three machine-guns had been kept trained on our cars in case they should stop, and would undoubtedly have killed us all had we turned back, while if we had gone on forward we would have fallen into enemy hands. The four of us stood behind the house, and the shooting continued. There was no one in the house.

'Where were you taking us?' I asked General Maslov, who was deathly pale. He did not reply, but his pallor changed into a blush of shame.

Zholudev answered for him: 'I said we weren't going the right way.'

As each of our divisions was advancing along separate lines there was no solid front line; we had gone through a gap between divisions. There was no sign of our troops and the enemy could easily make a sortie from his trenches to capture us. We must not delay and hang about behind this house. But what could we do? How could we break cover without being killed? We decided to crawl through the field of rye to the second house, about two hundred yards away, and then on to the next, a hundred and fifty yards further. We had to crawl flat among the short stalks of rye, keeping right down close to the ground.

It was very hot. Soaking in sweat and driven by fear we crawled on, oblivious to fatigue, hearing shots all the time though they were no longer aimed. Finally we got to within twenty-five yards of the second house, but were still separated from it by a potato field over which it was futile to crawl. We had a rest before making a dash for it, then set off and arrived together behind the house—the enemy had noticed us too late. In the same way we got to the next house. We were now five hundred yards from the enemy. Our fear of being captured had vanished, but not the fear of getting killed. We still had to cover five hundred yards to get to the forest or behind the hill. And that would not be easy: we would have to go up the slope in full view of the enemy. We decided to risk it, running quickly and with big gaps between us. After a short rest we set off. At first we came under machine-gun fire, and then shells and mortar bombs began to fall about us. The Germans had probably realised what big game was getting away—perhaps they had spotted three of us wearing red flashes.

Zholudev and Maslov chose a corner of the forest which jutted out towards us, although I tried to stop them by pointing out that the enemy probably had the range of the forest's edge. My orderly officer and I continued along the field aiming to find cover behind the crest of the hill. As soon as our comrades drew near the forest an artillery salvo rang out followed by about a dozen explosions along the forest's edge. I saw General Zholudev—a big man—tossed up in the air by an explosion and then fall. I knew he was past help.

When we were out of sight of the enemy and the firing had stopped I sent my orderly officer, I. A. Galushko, to the corner of the forest to find out what had happened. My car had been hit in several places but the driver and engine were undamaged. I followed my orderly officer in the car. When I saw him standing by the edge of the forest and signalling me to join him, I drove up. I had not been wrong. Galushko reported: 'When I got to the forest I first heard some groans and then found General Maslov unconscious and covered with earth. I picked him up, and then saw General Zholudev lying dead further on.'

We did not know where their orderly officers and the driver had got to. When the generals were making a dash for the house they had had time to shout to them: 'Get away as best you can.' It turned out that while the enemy's attention was entirely fixed on us they had got away to the forest. They emerged again when we called, helped to get Maslov into the car, put in Zholudev's body, and we slowly drove back to the headquarters of the 323rd Rifle Division.

Viktor Grigorevich Zholudev and the officers who were blown up in a minefield on the same day were buried at Volkovysk. The main street of this town was named after Zholudev.

In December, 1944, Marshal Rokossovskii, whom I already knew well from fighting side by side with him, was appointed commander of the 2nd Belorussian Front in the place of Army General G. F. Zakharov. By the time the advance began we had received from Front H.Q. many valuable instructions. For instance, in order to achieve surprise and economise on ammunition, we were told not to carry out reconnaissances in force the day before an attack, but to use assault battalions on the day during the first fifteen minutes of artillery preparation. Another instruction recommended that, because the enemy would probably only put up real resistance in his second line, we should capture the first line of defences by the fifteenth minute of artillery preparation. We received these instructions with special pleasure because our army had already put the first one into effect on its own initiative during the Bryansk operation and the second at the big attack when the bridge-head over the river Narev had been widened.

One thing distressed us. We counted on being reinforced by one of the tank corps but learned that the other armies advancing on our left had been given them, although they were advancing on a narrower front and had a rifle corps each in reserve; moreover, a complete tank army was being put in along their axis of advance. The 3rd Army not only had no tanks, it had no second echelon troops to develop its successes; all we had was an army reserve. And after our

advance our sector had widened out to twenty-eight miles.
To be honest, however, the front commander's decision,
which so annoyed us, was well founded. The armies on our
left were advancing in the more important west and north-
west directions, while we were advancing mainly north and
only partly to the north-west.

January 14th, 1945, dawned at last. The day was overcast
and misty, with visibility down to a hundred and fifty to
two hundred yards. This hindered observation and the full
use of our artillery, and grounded our pilots. We learned
later that the only reason for not postponing the attack
scheduled for this day was a request from our Western Allies,
who had raised the alarm because of an effective counter-
attack which the Germans had launched against them.

At exactly 1000 hours, artillery fire of unprecedented
power opened up along a wide front. Although we were
unable to spot bursts because of the mist we had full confidence in the excellent work of the gunners after their
thorough training. At the fifteenth minute they occupied the
first line of trenches with hardly any losses. By 1100 hours,
in spite of enemy fire, the sappers, together with the mine-
sweeping tanks, had cleared lanes for the infantry, and at
1110 hours, we had taken the second line along all its length.
Although the enemy threw in more troops and intensified
his fire, that day our troops advanced two to four miles
along the main axis and one to two miles along subsidiary
lines. During the night another three-quarters of a mile was
gained.

The next day, equally overcast, saw fighting of terrifying
power and bitterness. The enemy threw in all his reserves,
as well as the *Grosses Deutschland* Tank Division. Formerly this
formation had been operating on the southern border of
East Prussia in the area of Willenberg. It had not been

identified in our area by Intelligence. Taking advantage of
the poor visibility, however, it had in twenty-four hours
concentrated unnoticed in the area of our breakthrough
with the object of first retrieving the situation on our army's
front and then turning its attention to our neighbour to the
left.

We intended to renew the advance at 0900 hours but the
enemy forestalled us. He began his artillery counter-prepara-
tion at 0820 hours with fire from twenty-three artillery and
seventeen mortar batteries, a number of troops of six-
barrelled mortars and heavy rocket launches. At 0830 hours
he counter-attacked the forces which had penetrated his
defence. At noon a German tank division entered the battle.
By evening we had counted thirty counter-attacks. The
fighting died down only when darkness fell. Many inhabited
areas changed hands. We did not move forward but we did
not yield a yard although there were moments when the
tanks penetrated our fighting positions.

One tank group got within a hundred and fifty yards of
the knoll occupied by Corps Commander Nikitin. Not only
did he keep his observation point where it was but personally
directed the guns firing over open sights, to the great
inspiration of his gunners. Several heavy German tanks were
destroyed, others vanished back into the mist. I had always
known that General Nikitin was an excellent commander in
war, but I had no idea that there was so much strength and
energy in his small thin body, that this man had so much
daring and such reliance in his comrades-in-arms. Half an
hour later I was there, warmly thanking the gunners and
firmly embracing Nikitin.

The overcast weather on the second day was a vexation
not only for us: the pilots fretted at their inactivity. That
most experienced Air Force general, K. A. Vershinin, said to

me over the telephone: 'All the pilots are standing by their aircraft. They are eating their hearts out—but what can one do in weather like this?'

The enemy had succeeded in temporarily holding up our advance. But at what a price! Prisoners from the motorised regiment of the *Grosses Deutschland* Division reported that their regiment, which had been reinforced with seventy heavy 'Panther' and 'Tiger' tanks, had lost no less than a third of its tanks and personnel in the first three hours of the battle.

At dawn on January 16th fierce fighting started up again. We threw back counter-attacks, more than twenty of them, but during the second half of the day the weather cleared and with the help of the Air Force we advanced one or two miles. Air reconnaissance showed heavy German transport movement—vehicles and single tanks—to the west of us. After the failure of their counter-attacks and the threat from our advancing neighbours on the left, the enemy had begun to withdraw.

Every one of the unit commanders dreamed of being the first to cross the border of East Prussia. The honour fell to the 172nd Rifle Regiment, under the command of Lieutenant-Colonel Seregin, on January 20th, 1945. The Military Council of the Army congratulated the soldiers, sergeants and officers on their entry upon enemy territory in a proclamation which read: 'The desire that we have all shared for so long has been fulfilled. Now we must press on to the heart of Hitler's Germany and thrust into it our Red Army bayonet. Forward with all speed!'

We met hardly any civilians in the border area. Only decrepit old men and women, who wanted to die where they had been born, had stayed behind. The German troops and police drove out all those who did not want to leave.

These were mostly peasants, and whole families of them hid in the woods waiting for our troops. But the further we advanced into Germany the more civilians we met.

In Willenberg on the Omulev River the enemy held a prepared defence line with two trenches and a double row of wire. The town was burning—set on fire by the Germans themselves. We forced the river and by-passed the town to the east and west. The East Prussian town of Allenstein fell on January 22nd to units of the 3rd Guards Cavalry Corps and the 35th Rifle Corps.

We advanced more than sixty miles and accomplished in seven days the task of breaking through to the line Kline–Dankheim and Muschaken, a task for which we had been given eight days.

The next day, after advancing only two or three miles, we came across a fortified area constructed before the war, running north-west in our army sector. The enemy had fortified the shores of the lakes, which were high almost everywhere and covered with pine woods. In a number of places he had blown up dams and flooded low-lying areas and ravines.

The German Infantry General Gosbach ordered one group of his troops to break through to Elbing and another towards Allenstein. The push towards Elbing and the Bay failed. Only one escape route remained, over the ice, along the narrow tongue of land separating the Bay from the sea. This tongue of land, covered by forest, is two to two and a half miles wide and fifty miles long and terminates at Danzig (Gdansk). Prisoners told us that all the roads to the sea were jammed with military and civilian vehicles loaded with miscellaneous possessions, and that some of the soldiers were changing into civilian clothes in an attempt to get away into the heart of Germany, while others were looting valuables from the civilian population. The German troops were ordered to stand fast until the transport which had piled up on the roads had been cleared away. In this the enemy was able to take advantage of the many farmsteads in the area with their stone and brick buildings.

By February 1st our sector had narrowed sharply and we were fighting stubbornly for the town of Guttstadt. Our forces were badly depleted but in view of the high morale of our troops we decided to take the town at night. At 2300 hours, after a short artillery preparation, Captain Aleinik was the first to enter the town with an assault group. By 0300 hours next morning the enemy had been cleared out of the town.

In the pocket of a dead senior lieutenant we found a letter from an inhabitant of the town to Goebbels. Here it is in full:

'*To Reich Minister of Propaganda Dr. Goebbels,*
Berlin.

'I hope that these few lines will reach you. In the little town of Guttstadt we are going through something terrible. The chaos is worse than anything you can imagine. We need immediate help. I beg our Fuhrer for immediate help.

'The soldiers who pass here without their commanders are looting, changing into civilian clothes and throwing their uniforms into the streets. All their documents, equipment and helmets, everything which is connected with the army, has been thrown away and lies scattered around the houses. Everything looks as if the Russians had already done their job. All the streets are cluttered with ammunition, dead horses and foodstuffs, of which they had stolen so much that they were unable to take it all away. The local leader of the National Socialist Party, who is also the Buergermaster, has fled, leaving the civilian population to its fate.

'The soldiery, having lost its fear of the officers, has scattered. Those soldiers who are devoted to the Fuhrer are indignant at this behaviour. It seems that the officers have said to their men: "Work out for yourselves how best to get away from the Russians."

'Unfortunately, I cannot write any more. I want these lines to reach you. Good soldiers are helping me by taking this letter, and if they can, they will send it to your address.

'I believe in you. I want to remind you that I am an old member of the Party. Gauleiter Erich Koch knows me well.

Your faithful Party Comrade,
HILLI BORINSKI.'

The letter did not each its destination. We handed it instead to Ilya Grigorevich Ehrenburg who was with us then. He used it for an article in *Red Star*.

Infuriated by these defeats the Fuhrer replaced Gosbach, the commander of his 4th Army, and a number of the senior officers, accusing them of deliberately yielding Prussia to the Russians. Infantry General Muller took Gosbach's place. An order from Hitler was brought to the notice of every German soldier and officer stating that 'Every deserter is a traitor to the Fatherland. He will be shot and his family subjected to ruin and police action. Anyone who, not being wounded, becomes a prisoner of the Russians will be condemned to death and his family sent to hard labour or a concentration camp.' In his turn General Muller issued additional orders of great severity.

The Germans reinforced their operational divisions with everything they could lay hands on. Pamphlets were issued to the German troops by Hitler's High Command, proclaiming that 'the plans of the Bolsheviks have been wrecked. Powerful military forces have been built up in the German rear,' and so on. As a result of all this the enemy's resistance hardened. We noticed this during the next few days when we came to Wormditt and the outer ring of the Koenigsberg defences.

The Koenigsberg fortified area was laid out in the years between 1930 and 1934. It was the most powerful that we had seen up to that time. Apart from reinforced concrete pillboxes and armoured cupolas, joined by a network of trenches, there were dug-outs with heavy overhead cover, barbed wire several rows deep with rolls of wire between the rows and various well camouflaged obstacles. In front of the barbed wire there were anti-tank blocks, *chevaux-de-frise* and ditches. There were dense minefields in several places.

The steel doors of the pillboxes and shelters were a quarter of an inch thick, the reinforced concrete walls and ceilings were four and a half feet deep, and all the pillboxes were surrounded by electrified barbed wire. Sitting behind these fortifications the Hitlerites intended to cover the withdrawal of their troops from East Prussia.

Assessing the situation, we reckoned that our infantry was numerically equal to that of the enemy, that in terms of artillery and mortars we were significantly better off, but that we were markedly inferior to the enemy in tanks and armoured vehicles. Our indisputable superiority lay in the fact that the morale of our troops was excellent, while the Germans were catastrophically 'retreat-minded.'

We decided to take the 41st Corps out of the line and place it in reserve, so as to retain the means of developing a break-

through by the other two corps. We decided not to attack
every day but to marshal our strength and build up our
supplies of ammunition. We decided also to break through
on a narrow front.

Three days later, at dawn on February 5th, our files
approached the enemy's defence line through a ravine over-
grown with bushes and after a ten minute artillery preparation struck on the right flank. Because of the impetus and the
suddenness of the attack the Germans panicked. Our troops,
taking advantage of this, got across the tank ditches and
obstacles. The main force made for the forest; the rest with
their supporting artillery blockaded and destroyed the pillboxes on the outer edge of the perimeter. Such few tanks and
armoured vehicles as we had left overcame the tank ditches
and the minefields with the help of the sappers. At the forest
they joined the main infantry force. Soon a grim action was
raging in the pine forest which stretched over an area of
forty miles.

From an observation post on high ground one could see
our troops pouring into the forest. An hour of continuous
fighting went by. We had no means of telling what was
happening. From reports we learned only of the liquidation
of pillboxes on the forward edge. When these had been
finished off the second echelon moved towards the forest and
also disappeared into it. Only by morning did we capture
the whole forest and emerge at the river Drewenz, where we
met a new line of defence.

The next day units under the bold General Telkov and the
prudent Colonel Abilov were the first to force the Drewenz
and drive a wedge into the next defence area. During these
two days we drove back more than thirty counter-attacks.

The enemy took advantage of the dense network of good
roads and quickly threw in his reserves wherever we seemed

certain of success. On February 7th we only repelled attacks and did not advance. As we were short of shells and mortar ammunition I was compelled to instruct formation commanders, once they had found suitable positions, to repel attacks by means of small arms only and to use artillery and mortars only at short range, when the effect was certain.

The Germans attacked continuously for two days, suffering heavy losses, but nowhere were they able to drive us back. Our losses were smaller and we did not retreat. On the third day there was a short pause. We took advantage of this to bring up ammunition, to comb through once more whatever was left in the rear and make up our undermanned units with our findings.

By now the 2nd Belorussian Front was already facing due west and our army, being on the right flank, was transferred to the 3rd Belorussian Front, commanded by Army General Chernyakhovski.

He came to see us in Freimark the next day. It was the first time I had met him. He was very young, energetic and confident. As soon as we met he expressed great satisfaction with the practical instructions given to formation commanders. I remember his words: 'That's fine. Very correct.' He again expressed satisfaction when he heard my assessment of the situation and a report of our intentions. He asked me how old I was and what I had commanded before the war.

'Fifty-four years old. I commanded a division,' I answered.

He moved away a little, looked me over and said: 'That's fine too.'

Then he asked the name of the divisional commander whom he had met on the road. I had some difficulty in answering, not knowing whom he meant. He described him. 'He is quite an old man,' he said.

'There are no old men among the divisional commanders,' I told him.

'Well, he would be about forty-five.'

'If he were playing with dolls at forty-five,' I said, 'he would be a little old for it, but that's still not a great age for commanding a division.' I added: 'In 1914 when the Germans were enveloping Paris the flanking armies were commanded by Bulow and Kluck; one was sixty-seven and the other was sixty-nine, and they both commanded well.'

After this conversation, Army General Chernyakhovski became more formal with me. But how about that—an old man!

After General Chernyakhovski's death the combined command of the 3rd White Russian and 1st Baltic Fronts was taken over by Marshal of the Soviet Union A. M. Vasilevski, the Chief of the General Staff. Vasilevski was only in Moscow when big operations were being prepared and spent the rest of his time with the troops in the field helping the commanders and directing them.

I had seen Aleksandr Mikhailovich Vasilevski in Stalingrad in the autumn of 1942 and he had impressed me as a general of outstanding ability and at the same time an exceptionally modest and charming man.

Immediately after his appointment Vasilevski visited us, greeted all those who were present in the command post and said to them: 'I met your commander in Stalingrad—he was walking about one dark night outside the town and I gave him a lift in my car.'

Our advance was slow. The enemy's resistance grew as his hope of victory or a peace which would preserve the Fascist State diminished. The soldiers who regarded themselves merely as involuntary participants in the war deserted, but there were many at the front who felt a share of responsibility in it and were afraid that they would have to pay for their crimes. The front continued to shrink and the enemy tightened his defence. We were hindered by the weather, which was not suitable for flying, and without air reconnaissance we had little information about the enemy. The ground was flat, intersected by woods, villages and farmsteads. In order to observe anything at all of the enemy positions in depth we had to erect watch towers to the height of the highest trees at every second mile of our advance. Even from these, however, little could be seen because of the mist.

Out of the woods there emerged to meet us one by one or in groups Soviet women who had been driven off to work from the areas of Leningrad, Pskov, Novgorod, Smolensk and from White Russia and the Ukraine. I cannot describe how glad they were at the possibility of returning home, and yet they were going back to places which had been looted and burned to the ground by the Germans.

I had remembered well the lessons about economy learned from my regimental commander in 1914, and issued an order to collect and preserve the cattle and property which the fleeing Germans had abandoned. By March 1st we had gathered 29,240 head of long-horned cattle—the unmilked cows, which were lowing in pain, were milked by soldiers! —890 pigs, 6,000 sheep and 3,100 tons of grain.

After a short rest and regrouping we concentrated our troops on a front line three miles wide, so that our infantry was double the enemy strength and our artillery and mortars were five times more numerous. We only had eighteen tanks and armoured vehicles, however. On March 14th we opened our attack and in three days managed to advance three miles, occupying two enemy defence areas. To achieve this our army had to drive a deep wedge into the enemy's positions.

thus coming under fire not only from the front but from the flanks.

Fortunately on March 18th and 19th the weather was suitable for flying. Our Air Force helped us to take the motor highway in the enemy's rear, which had served him as an excellent line of communication for the movement of his reserves. In these two days of flying the Air Force not only helped the troops on the ground to advance, but it obtained vital information about enemy groupings in depth. During these two days our troops advanced another three miles, which at that stage represented a great success. We were now only three or four miles from the Bay. The enemy's last defence area passed near the town of Heiligenbeil and the railway from it to Braunsberg was jammed tight with trucks. This was carried in a night attack on March 25th. That same day General Urbanovich's corps reached the Frisches Haff. By dawn the whole army was on its shore.

The morning of March 26th was quiet and sunny. The silence was broken by the firing of single guns—snipers firing at barges and rafts as they sailed away. Machine-guns fired at smaller targets, men trying to avoid capture by using improvised craft. Our aircraft, in neat formations, were bombing the narrow tongue of land visible in the distance.

And what a scene there was on the shore of the Bay! An area of several square miles was entirely covered with cars and vehicles loaded with military equipment, provisions and chattels. Between the cars and vehicles lay the bodies of German soldiers. Horses were tied in lines of two or three hundred, and remained tied even after they had been killed.

Early that morning I saw on the shore boxes of foodstuffs and bags of coffee used as cover, built into the parapets of the trenches. In places I was reminded of what we had seen in the way of German possessions when we freed Stalingrad. Sometimes this scene even exceeded it in strangeness. By that time almost all of Germany was starving, and yet here there were plenty of supplies.

I called Marshal Vasilevski and invited him down: 'To believe it you must see it with your own eyes.' Three hours later Aleksandr Mikhailovich arrived, congratulated the troops and added: 'This must be recorded for your offspring.'

The Political Department shot a film of the Hitlerite rout, which was later presented to the Museum of the Soviet Army. As he was leaving for Koenigsberg, Vasilevski said: 'Now have a rest. You have honestly deserved it.'

But soldiers from the crowd shouted to him: 'To Berlin! To Berlin!'

That day was a happy one, shared by all. Moscow saluted us and we joined it in treating ourselves to a salute all the evening. Rockets soared into the sky right up to midnight. There was not a shot fired anywhere along the whole of our army's front.

From March 27th, for the first time in the war, the army was neither engaging with the enemy nor busy with a military task. We were in reserve. The trophy detachment worked ceaselessly, unloading and sorting what they took from the road convoys and storehouses. Everybody—riflemen, gunners, sappers and signalmen—willingly gave them a hand.

In all the headquarters the accounts for the last two days and for the operation as a whole were made up. The balance sheet proved highly satisfactory.

TWELVE

Victory

As we were now in the G.H.Q. reserve we reckoned on ten to fifteen days to make up our ranks and put ourselves in order. However, already on April 1st we received a directive to transfer to the north-east of Frankfurt-on-Oder.

We were not upset by this; in fact we were rather pleased, because everyone wanted to take part in the battle for Berlin. We were disturbed at our shortage of men, but we hoped for the best and believed that we would receive reinforcements before going into action. Nor were we mistaken; when we arrived in our new area of concentration we did receive some small reinforcements. Awards were given to many and proclamations read awarding the title of Hero of the Soviet Union to many, including myself.

I reported to the commander of the 1st Belorussian Front, Marshal G. K. Zhukov, and informed him of progress in concentrating the army. He told me that the attack on Berlin was to begin long before dawn, by the light of one hundred and forty-five searchlights which would blind the enemy and turn night into day. He said that four mixed and two tank armies would attack along a front from a bridge-head fifteen miles wide. He told us of the measure which would be taken to draw the enemy off from the direction of Berlin. It would be taken on the fifth day and we would reach the Elbe on April 26th.

I expressed the fear that an attack at night in such close

order would lead to confusion among formations and units. And why turn night into day? Would it not be better to wait until dawn? I also thought, although I kept the thought to myself, that the formations on the bridge-head were too closely packed and that it was unreasonable to try to take Berlin by storm. It would be better to blockade it and march to the Elbe.

In his conversation with me the front commander held to his opinion about a night attack. As it turned out, however, the attack did not begin at night but at 0630 hours.

Having reached the Oder and the Neisse and seized the bridge-heads, the troops of the front began to prepare for the Berlin operation. By April 15th, when our army, with the exception of some rear units moving in their own time, was concentrating in the second echelon of the 1st Belorussian Front, the preparations were already completed. Two of our divisions were placed in defence facing the enemy bridge-head on the eastern bank of the Oder, opposite Frankfurt-on-Oder.

The German Command clearly expected our attack any day. It had succeeded in creating a fixed defence on both rivers—a deep defence area with intermediary zones and cut-off positions. There was a particularly strong defence position in front of the Kuestrin bridge-head on the Seelow heights. Their ridge was about three miles from our forward zone and from it the enemy could overlook the whole bridge-head. Opposite the British and Americans the Germans did not create any defence areas between Berlin and the Elbe.

The approach to Berlin was defended by Army Group 'Weissel' formed from the 3rd Tank and 9th Armies and also elements of Army Group 'Zenter,' a total of up to sixty divisions with innumerable individual supporting units. Apart from this in Berlin itself, surrounded by three defence

areas, up to two hundred separate battalions were formed.
The Germans dismantled the whole of their Reserve Army,
all military training establishments and all Higher Military
Academies, and used the personnel to man the units at the
front, thereby bringing them up to seventy and eighty per
cent. of establishment, and to form separate battalions. They
took formations from the Western Front with no fears about
leaving it bare, and transferred them to the east. Hitler had
still not lost hope of concluding a separate compromise peace
with the British and Americans.

The task of breaking through the enemy defence on the
Oder and Neisse, of dismembering and destroying this
powerful force, was entrusted by our Supreme Command to
the troops of the 1st Belorussian, 1st Ukrainian and 2nd
Belorussian Fronts.

The 1st Belorussian Front went into action on April 16th.
The defence was pierced. By the 22nd our line of the front
passed through the northern suburbs of Greater Berlin and
on round through Strausberg, Kinbaum, Buchholz, Belen-
dorf, to the northern outskirts of Frankfurt. At the same time
the leading formations of the 1st Ukrainian Front were
approaching the outskirts of Greater Berlin, by-passing the
Frankfurt–Guben enemy grouping from the south and south-
west.

By this time our army had concentrated and received its
task: to attack in the area Schoenfeld–Kagel–Bondsdorf,
and, on the left, Heinersdorf–Buchholz–Bindow–Mitten-
walde; to make contact with a formation of the 1st Ukrainian
Front, complete the encirclement and cut off the line of
retreat of the Frankfurt–Guben group to Berlin; then to
destroy it, jointly with our neighbours. The army of Colonel-
General Chuikov was attacking to our right and the army of
Colonel-General Kolpakchi to our left.

The decision to complete the encirclement of the enemy grouping was taken by us in the ancient castle of Jansfolde. Its witnesses were the ancestral owners of the castle and the rulers whom they had revered. They eyed us with a glazed look from the gilded frames on the walls of the vast library.

We considered that the morale of the enemy was shattered and that the German soldiers would show fight only from fear of being shot by their own punitive detachments. It was therefore thought more profitable to attack at night, when officers have less control over their men, particularly in wooded country. We decided to force the Spree and the Oder-Spree canal during the night of the 23rd, to push the attack and, by April 25th, to break out on to the Berlin–Zossen highway, having completed the encircling movement. This was a difficult task, bearing in mind not only the distance—twenty-two miles—but also the large lakes with narrow tongues of land between, themselves intersected by shipping canals. However, the task was accomplished on time. It is true that we met with organised resistance but it was not what it had been earlier in East Prussia. The fiercest fighting began when we had closed the ring and set about destroying the groups we had surrounded.

As we advanced we captured an area of age-old pines and many beautiful houses on the banks of the lakes. For centuries the German nobility had lived here, and later Hitler's retainers. The servants who had remained in the villas and houses hung out white flags. Often we came upon Hitlerites who had committed suicide, some by hanging and some by shooting. Sometimes whole families had been shot. Fanatical Fascists had killed their wives and children before killing themselves.

At Neue-Mole we captured the powerful Berlin radio station in full working order, with part of its personnel who offered us their services. We captured a factory which made explosives and other factories with their equipment in good repair.

At dawn on April 30th, we heard the artillery of the armies of Generals Kolpakchi and Tsvetaev. The surrounded group of Germans had ceased to exist as a military force.

That day was marked by three events. The Red Flag was raised over the Reichstag, Hitler committed suicide and the troops of the 1st Ukrainian Front met the Americans on the Elbe.

On May 1st we were ordered to concentrate on the northern boundary of Berlin to strike at the surrounded enemy garrison. But during the night the Berlin garrison capitulated and we were sent to the Elbe, a distance of seventy-five miles. We reckoned that we could cover the distance in three days and prevent Hitler's troops from escaping to the British and Americans.

I was with one of the divisions that pursued the German troops as they retreated in a north-westerly direction to the Elbe, and I saw not only the surrounded Germans crowding together on the bank but also how they tried to get across the river by every sort of means—on steamers, barges, motor boats and pleasure boats, even individuals swimming in their underclothes in spite of the cold. I contacted the commander of the American 102nd Infantry Division and the commander of an infantry regiment on the opposite bank, asking them to return the Germans who had crossed to their side. My request was based on the fact that we could have fired at those Germans and sunk their craft but had not done so for fear of hitting our Allies. The commander of the 102nd Infantry Division, Major-General Kitinch, agreed with my motives and returned a large group of Germans to us together with the ships and barges. In the name of the army, and from myself personally I conveyed our thanks to the American troops and to Kitinch. This was greeted by cheering from the Americans on the far bank.

On the evening of May 9th the officers of the Army Head-quarters together celebrated the day of victory by a supper. I have mentioned that in 1907 I vowed never to smoke, drink or swear. All my life people have pestered me and tried to persuade me to drink, particularly in wartime. Once I was reckless enough to say: 'I'll drink when we win the war.' I had forgotten about this, but my comrades had not. The whole assembly insisted that I should keep my word. Our supper was held in the flowering garden of one of the most beautiful houses in Brandenburg West. That evening, to the delighted cheers of my comrades, I broke one of my three vows.

70
71
72
74
75
76
77
79
81
83
85
88